Second Playbill Two

The *Playbill* series brings together new, specially commissioned or adapted plays for use in schools. The emphasis is on contemporary developments in the theatre and allied media. The volumes are graded in difficulty.

Books by Alan Durband

ENGLISH WORKSHOP 1–3
CONTEMPORARY ENGLISH 1–2
SHORTER CONTEMPORARY ENGLISH
NEW ENGLISH 1–4

Edited by Alan Durband

NEW DIRECTIONS
(Five one-act plays in the modern idiom)
PLAYBILL 1–3
SECOND PLAYBILL 1–3

Edited by Alan Durband

SECOND
PLAYBILL TWO

Hutchinson Educational

HUTCHINSON EDUCATIONAL LTD
3 Fitzroy Square, London W1

London Melbourne Sydney Auckland
Wellington Johannesburg Cape Town
and agencies throughout the world

First published January 1973

This selection © Alan Durband 1973

*This book has been set in Bembo type, printed in Great Britain
on smooth wove paper by Anchor Press, and
bound by Wm. Brendon, both of Tiptree, Essex*

ISBN 0 09 113490 0 (c)
0 09 113491 9 (p)

Contents

Introduction	7
Acknowledgements	13
Words CECIL TAYLOR	15
Cabbages GAIE HOUSTON	43
The Singing Door DORIS LESSING	69
Burn-up DEREK BOWSKILL	99
Weevils in My Biscuit CHARLES SAVAGE	127

Introduction

Second Playbill Two contains plays by Cecil Taylor, Gaie Houston, Doris Lessing, Derek Bowskill and Charles Savage.

1 *The Plays*

Cecil Taylor's *Words* is about the generation gap. Mr Campbell believes that a man is as old as he feels, thinks and dresses. He's an individualist. It doesn't bother him when children mock as he runs through the streets with his son, Bob. The main thing is that he's proving his point: common interests cut across age groups. And when he rents an old shop, he has the best of motives. He doesn't want to impose anything on his son's pals, or to intrude upon them as a group. He merely wants to get a good idea off the ground. He wants to use the old head on his shoulders and his modest capital to give the younger generation a place they can call their own—where he can drop in now and again as a change from his wage-earning life as a respectable salesman. The teenagers don't have to help him decorate the premises, but when he finds them a job so that Martin can fix his car, they feel they owe him a debt of gratitude. Tensions develop within the group. Loyalties are stretched. There are disappointments and disillusionments. Perhaps there are two worlds after all, as Kate says, and each must have its own way of life.

Gaie Houston's *Cabbages* is another play in which there is conflict between the generations. It grew from the author's involvement with an acting group consisting entirely of young people. One of them happened to say that the older generation doesn't think, doesn't feel, doesn't imagine, but just kicks kids around until they conform and become cabbage-heads. The play that developed is a satire on conventional thinking and traditional approaches to life. The Head's curriculum is based on the values of a competitive society, represented here by the self-made man and Chairman of the Education Committee, Mr Hodge. Miss Fitt, so appropriately named, is a teacher professionally committed to turning out conformists. Anthony, with the biggest cabbage on his head, is the orthodox system's bright boy. But left alone, and under the influence of think-music, the boys and girls find their own personal identities. They offer an alternative to the world of 'suffering and struggle and disappointment and failure' which their education has prepared them for.

Doris Lessing's *The Singing Door* is also set in a community whose stability depends on rigid rules and regulations. It is a sub-world of advanced gadgetry on the one hand, and traditional myth on the other. Its life is sustained by means of Article 17 of their Declaration of Faith, which says that one day the Door around which their culture is built will open, and the people will reach 'the open air and the light of day' —concepts spoken of with religious awe but little understanding. This elaborate civilisation, subject to political upheavals like any other, is skilfully capable of maintaining itself from generation to generation. Its orthodoxy is so stifling that it entangles itself in its own rituals, terminology and beliefs. Prisoners of pettiness and ignorance, the elders let opportunities pass by that others, in their simplicity and faith, can seize. Clearly there is a message in this religious and political allegory for modern man.

Introduction

The play that follows deals with a related question. In an age of living for kicks, what is the nature of the fuel that can really be relied upon to keep the fire of life going? Derek Bowskill's *Burn-up* is an imaginative exploration of experience. His chorus have been everywhere, seen everything, done the lot—only to discover that the fire they are seeking cannot be sustained. Eventually they learn that 'it is in the heart of men like Schweitzer where the fire is', and that 'if what you want is Fire, then get burning, man. Burn inside. 'Cos that's for real.'

Burn-up is a play involving a large cast willing to experiment with rhythm and vocal music. It provides ample scope for mime and improvisation. *Weevils in My Biscuit* by Charles Savage is in a similar idiom. It depends on teamwork and discipline for its dramatic success. A naval revue, it shoots out a load of historical information, a lot of it light-hearted and amusing. All of it is true. It sets out to discover when the legend of the first navy in the world began. The author believes it was in the eighteenth century, when Britannia ruled the waves on ships notorious for their terrible conditions, brutality, mutinies, disease, desertions, and press-gangings. The script is functional and direct, with a good deal of authentic documentation. It can be taken as a complete unit, or regarded as the first act of two—the second being an improvised programme about life on board an eighteenth-century man-of-war. There is little need for further historical evidence—there is enough in Act One to excite the imagination.

2 The Playwrights

Cecil Taylor was born in Glasgow in 1929. He left school at

fourteen and worked at various jobs—electrician, radio engineer, television engineer, charity worker, and commercial traveller. He began writing poetry in 1944, then short stories, mostly for the Anglo-Jewish press. Eventually he turned to plays, and with *Mr David* won second prize in the World Jewish Congress Playwriting Competition. Since then he has written many television plays, including some for schools television, a film script, and a number of full-length plays, including *The Rise and Fall of Joe Soap*, *Happy Days are Here Again*, *Allergy*, and *Bread and Butter*. He lives in Northumberland.

Gaie Houston was born in London in 1933, and brought up in Nottinghamshire. She went to Newark Girls' High School and Oxford University. She has worked as a waitress, a teacher, and the manager of a psychiatric hospital. In 1969, in Florida, she says she 'came to life'. She now writes plays, mostly for radio, and works in the Encounter Group Movement.

Doris Lessing was born in Persia in 1919, where her father worked in the Imperial Bank. In 1924 her family moved to Southern Rhodesia, farming an area that was by British standards very rough and wild. She had a very inadequate schooling until she was fourteen, and then educated herself through reading, and knowing a great many people, most of whom would be regarded in this country as eccentric. In 1949 she moved to London. Her chief works are *Children of Violence*, a sequence of five novels the writing of which took twenty years, *The Golden Notebook*, several collections of stories and short novels, two full-length stage plays, *Play With a Tiger* and *The Truth about Billy Newton*, and various television plays.

Introduction

Derek Bowskill was born in Lincolnshire in 1928. Educated at Brigg Grammar School and Sheffield University, he completed his training at the Rose Bruford School of Speech and Drama before spending several years as a teacher. In 1955 he was appointed Drama Adviser to Devon Education Committee, and twelve years later moved to Eastbourne to take up a post as Head of the Department of Drama, Film and TV at the College of Education there. He has subsequently been Director of Research for Theatre Centre, and in 1970 he visited America and Canada on a universities lecture tour. He is Vice-Chairman of the National Drama Conference, and his works include *Drama Workshop* (for the BBC), and a sixty-minute documentary film, *Drama and Theatre in Education*. He has also written a number of children's and adults' plays, and several have been translated.

Charles Savage was born in 1944. Educated at Bradfield College and London University, he trained for the theatre at the Central School of Speech and Drama. For two years he was Assistant Director at the new Northcott Theatre, Exeter, and for a further two, Associate Director at Nottingham Playhouse. He has also written *Bottom* ('a scandalous review of eighteenth-century morals'), *Oh Soldier Soldier* (an examination of wars and why we fight), *X is a Comedy*, and *Cage* (a pop version of Shakespeare's *Othello*). His interests include mountaineering, fishing, Rugby and cricket, fast 1930's motor cars, wine and music. One of his ambitions is to direct a theatre company 'as far from London as possible'.

Acknowledgements

For permission to publish the plays in this volume, the editor is grateful to the following authors and their agents: Cecil Taylor, Clive Goodwin Associates, and BBC Schools Television for *Words*; Gaie Houston and Hughes Massie Ltd for *Cabbages*; Doris Lessing and Jonathan Clowes Ltd for *The Singing Door*; Derek Bowskill and Curtis Brown Ltd for *Burn-up*; Charles Savage and Felix de Wolfe Ltd for *Weevils in My Biscuit*.

No performance of these plays may be given unless a licence has been obtained. Applications should be addressed to the authors' agents.

Words

CECIL TAYLOR

CAST

BOB
MR CAMPBELL
MRS CAMPBELL
KATE
DAVE
LOUISE
MARTIN

All applications to perform this play, whether by amateurs or professionals, should be addressed to Clive Goodwin Associates, Cromwell Road, London SW7

DEDICATION

In remembrance of my father,
Max George Taylor

Words

SCENE 1: *A street.* BOB *and his father,* MR CAMPBELL, *in track suits, are running side by side. A group of kids at a corner cheers them on as they pass.*

BOB: It's probably running through the streets, that does it, Da . . . You reckon . . .

MR CAMPBELL: What I'm saying, Bob . . . Is if you don't want to do it, son . . . If it doesn't turn you on any more. You know . . .

BOB: Da . . . If I didn't want to . . . I wouldn't . . . I mean . . . If we were on a track . . .

MR CAMPBELL: If you take your own road, Bob . . . There's always people'll take you for a head case . . .

BOB: It's the street . . . I'm just working it out . . . You know . . . They think we're nut cases because we run through the streets . . . I was trying to work it out . . . They don't know you're my father, too . . . That's another thing . . .

MR CAMPBELL: Yes . . . Could be . . . Does it bother you? These characters . . . Doesn't bother me.

BOB: Doesn't bother me, Dad . . . Just a laugh . . .

MR CAMPBELL: What I'm getting at . . . Is we should only do things like this together . . . If we're still both getting kicks out of it . . . You know . . . I mean . . . If it's a drag . . .

Breaking away from your mates . . . To come back here for a workout . . . Is it?

BOB: . . . What?

MR CAMPBELL: Sometimes a drag? . . . Coming back in time?

BOB: It's only a couple of nights a week . . . Café closes at ten anyway, doesn't it?

MR CAMPBELL: What I'm sayin', son . . . Is it doesn't matter . . . You see. If you've a great scene going with your mates . . . And you don't want to up and go and leave it . . . See what I mean?

BOB: Yeah, Dad . . . Got the message . . . Sure . . .

MR CAMPBELL: . . . Turn down this road . . .

BOB: . . . Different way, tonight? . . .

MR CAMPBELL: . . . Something to show you . . .

SCENE 2: *A café.*

KATE: You're not serious, are you, Martin?

DAVE: Just a laugh, Kate.

KATE: What for?

MARTIN: Curiosity. I want to see it. Bobby and Daddy running round the block hand in hand.

KATE: Honestly, Martin. That's pathetic, isn't it?

LOUISE: I couldn't do it, even if I wanted to, Martin. It's silly. Honestly. It's just dead childish.

DAVE: It's a laugh, Louise!

KATE: What you trying to prove like, Martin? Apart from the fact you don't like him?

LOUISE: He does, Kate.

MARTIN: Don't like him, don't dislike him. That's what I'm on about. Does nothing to us.

DAVE: Good thing, mind. Getting himself trained. That's alright.

KATE: I mean, what will that do? We all go round to the house, and cheer them on their run . . . I mean . . . Can you see yourself really doing it? Going out, and when his Dad and him come round . . .

MARTIN: It's just sick, Kate. It annoys us . . .

LOUISE: I think it's great, being able to do things like with your father. Isn't it, Kate?

MARTIN: He's your man, Kate, isn't he? If you're happy with him still having to play with Daddy like that . . .

KATE: I don't have any man! What you on about?

DAVE: *You* brought him along to the café, Kate.

LOUISE: He is a bit, isn't he, Kate?

KATE: What does that mean? A bit?

MARTIN: Alright. He's nobody's man but his Daddy's . . .

KATE: Don't be bloody pathetic, Martin. For God's sake. We're supposed to be on about trying to get some money for your new crankshaft, aren't we? That's always what happens when we try to get something organised. You and Dave go off at all angles.

DAVE: Bob went off in the middle of organising it, Kate, didn't he?

LOUISE: I've seen his father. I think he's nice.

MARTIN: Great. You go runnin' with him, too . . .

KATE: We need fifteen quid for a new crankshaft.

DAVE: Bob reckons his Dad might come up with an idea to raise the cash.

LOUISE: I've got about three pound. I'm saving for a coat.

DAVE: Are we going or not?

KATE: I've never seen his Dad. You fancy him, Louise?

DAVE: Here's your chance. We'll go and catch up with them.

MARTIN [*to the girls*]: Dave, man. They've spoiled it. You hold us back. You definitely hold us back. Whenever we want to go wild . . . You stop us . . .

KATE: You know what to do about that, don't you?

MARTIN: I mean, sometimes you fancy acting daft, don't you, Dave, man?

SCENE 3: *The old shop.*

MR CAMPBELL: What do you think of it?

BOB: Great. What you going to do with it, Dad?

MR CAMPBELL: Thought of using it, at first, as a storehouse for the firm. Extra depot.

BOB: Hey, it's big, isn't it?

MR CAMPBELL: Then I gave myself a shake. I'm tied up enough with flogging tinned meat and soup. That shows you how involved I get, flogging, doesn't it? Get a chance of a place like this, and the first thing I think of is taking it over for the firm!

BOB: It's big.

MR CAMPBELL: Could dance in here easily, couldn't you?

BOB: Great!

MR CAMPBELL: I mean, living in two worlds—parents and kids—that's finished, now isn't it, Bob?

BOB: I never think about it, Dad.

MR CAMPBELL: I mean. Age. Physical age . . . I'm thirty-eight. You're seventeen. But I can out-run you, any time, can't I?

BOB: I don't know, Dad.

MR CAMPBELL: What I'm saying is, it doesn't mean anything, does it? I have no age. I'm a kid, too, when it comes down to it, aren't I?

BOB: I'm telling you, Dad. I never think about it. I just think about you . . . just like a mate. And my mother . . .

MR CAMPBELL: A place like this. The kids are crying out for a place like this on the estate. Just for themselves. To do their own things in it. See what I mean? See, there's a yard outside. Make it into a football pitch. Tennis, maybe.

BOB: It's great, Dad.

MR CAMPBELL: When it's all done, it'll belong to the kids. You could call it something like 'OURS'. Get a coffee machine. Record player. Paint in it. Make things. Poetry readings. Anything you fancy.

BOB: Have we got it, Dad?

MR CAMPBELL: This is your place, if you want it. No strings. I'm paying the rent. It's hardly anything anyway.

BOB: It's great, Dad.

MR CAMPBELL: What I'll do is, I'll make a start. Maybe get a mate or two of mine along. If any of your mates drop in and fancy taking up a brush—great! I mean, that's the only way to do it, Bob. The only way to break down these barriers is to work together for some common aim.

BOB: Yeah, Dad . . . Hey. If we have this shop, maybe we could have a jumble sale or something. To raise the money to fix Martin's car . . .

MR CAMPBELL [*locking up*]: Yeah. What's this problem with Martin's car? [*Trotting off*] Tell me about it. Maybe we'll be able to organise something for him . . .

SCENE 4: *Outside a multi-storey block of flats. Advertising material is being distributed.*

DAVE: If we don't go and play with your Dad in this shop he's got, like, he'll not get us any more jobs like this . . .

BOB: I'm just telling you about it, Dave. It's nothing to him if you go or don't . . .

LOUISE: If we kept all these . . . '2$\frac{1}{2}$p off Ten Fish Fingers' . . . and 'Angel Delight' . . .

KATE [*to Bob*]: But it's something to you, isn't it, if we go or we don't go?

LOUISE: I mean, going round *all these doors*!

MARTIN: They check, Louise. You've got to give them out.

KATE [*to Bob*]: Isn't it, Bob?

DAVE: I'm keeping some of them. Keeping the fish fingers.

LOUISE: I don't see how they can. How can they check?

BOB [*to Kate*]: Why should it be anything to me, like? What are you on about now, Kate?

MARTIN: Your sick father, man.

BOB: You've never bloody seen him.

KATE: Bloody *heard* about him. Haven't we?

DAVE: No, got us this job. If he wouldn't have got us this job, we'd've been without transport. And we could'ne done a job like this . . . without transport . . . See what I mean?

BOB: Hilarious!

LOUISE: I can't see how they check . . .

MARTIN: For God's sake somebody tell Louise how they check! They do, Louise.

BOB: They've got market research people.

KATE: They definitely know if you don't give them out. Girl I knew got a job pushing out stuff like that, and she got so sick, she stuffed half of it down the loo. She never got asked again to do it.

BOB: They check. My Dad warned us. I mean . . . Bothering . . . When Martin's car needs fixing . . . And things like that . . . And this place . . . It's smashing . . . I just think . . . I don't . . . I mean . . . Your own father didn't do anything to help you get your car fixed, did he?

MARTIN: I'm saying . . . Bob's father's a great man. The greatest!

DAVE: Got a yard outside, this place he's got?

BOB: I told you.

KATE: Why does he bother, like?

LOUISE: He fancies doing it. Why shouldn't he . . .

KATE: I hate painting, anyway. Or anything like that.

MARTIN: Hate anything that looks like work, you!

DAVE: I fancy the yard. Make it into a netball court. You know? And I fancy painting . . . Like slobbing on paint . . .

BOB: Great. If you fancy going along . . . Go along . . . If you don't . . . It doesn't matter.

KATE: Matters to you . . .

MARTIN: I've enough fathers of my own, Bob, man. I don't want to get lumbered with other people's.

LOUISE: Let's get on with this. The sooner we start . . . the sooner we'll be finished. [*Handing Martin a pile, angrily*]

MARTIN: That's what he's doing, isn't it? Lumbering us with his father.

KATE: I mean that name . . .

DAVE: It's alright.

BOB: It's just something he threw at us . . . You can call it anything.

KATE: 'OURS.' That's really *sick!*

MARTIN: Real sick!

BOB [*bursts out in anger*]: Look! If you don't get on with your people, that's you, isn't it? This is me. I just don't have any problems with my father or my mother . . .

LOUISE: That's stupid. You're right, Bob. Making out there's something wrong with Bob because he can have his father for a friend!

KATE: We're not saying that, Louise.

DAVE: I'm game to try it, Bob, man. I fancy it . . .

BOB: What are you saying, then, Kate?

KATE: I don't know what I'm saying . . . You can't know what you're saying all the time. Louise, give us my quota, and let's get started . . .

SCENE 5: BOB's *house*. MR CAMPBELL *is putting on a new, swinging leather jacket. He is wearing tight-fitting cords. His wife watches him.*

MRS CAMPBELL [*admiring him*]: Honest . . . I think you should!

MR CAMPBELL: I'm tied enough during the day, with a collar and tie, and my commercial traveller's bloody suit, Sue . . .

MRS CAMPBELL: I'm just jealous. I wish I had the courage to wear mini dresses up to my thighs, and nine-inch false eyelashes . . .

MR CAMPBELL: That's what I feel like. You see, I don't feel like a collar-and-tie lounge-suited representative for bloody canned foods!

MRS CAMPBELL [*taking his hands*]: I know, pet.

MR CAMPBELL: I don't feel old. I don't feel any age. You don't. Nothing to stop you wearing what you fancy, either, is there?

MRS CAMPBELL: So long as I wear them indoors . . .
[MR CAMPBELL *is getting his painting gear together*]

MRS CAMPBELL: Ralph, honey, if you're going to paint . . .

MR CAMPBELL [*showing her*]: I've got overalls.

MRS CAMPBELL: You think Bob'll *turn* up with his friends to help?

MR CAMPBELL: If they want. If they want . . .

MRS CAMPBELL: Do you not think, maybe, you're a wee bit kind of *forcing* yourself . . . [*Withdraws at the utterance*] I don't know . . .

MR CAMPBELL [*this is a sore point*]: I told you, it's up to them. If they want to come, they'll come. If they don't want to use it, there's plenty of other kids'll take it. You've just got to go ahead and do what you want to do, Sue, haven't you? I mean, I've got to keep looking round my shoulder at what other people's thinking of us all day, haven't I? 'Better watch myself with this character; or he'll drop his order this visit.' Now I'm doing what I fancy doing. I'm going to try and organise this place for the kids. If Bob wants to help. Great.

MRS CAMPBELL [*kissing him*]: Ralph, you look great, honestly. It's just . . . You know . . . You sometimes wonder . . . How you look to Bob . . . and the rest of the kids . . . But that's stupid, isn't it?

MR CAMPBELL [*going*]: That's how I feel like. [*Indicating his gear*] Isn't it? If I'm going to start worrying about what other people think about my gear . . .

SCENE 6: *The café.*

KATE: I'm just daft, Bob. Don't listen to me.

BOB: It doesn't matter. Kate . . . I just thought . . . You know . . . I fancied coming over for you . . . That's all.

KATE: It was just me giving you what I should have given to my Dad, Bob. Told you I'm stupid. I should be dead glad you came for me. It was nice . . .

BOB: It doesn't bother me . . . If you don't fancy going tonight, Kate . . . I'm easy . . .

KATE: Bob, don't do that. That's stupid. I hate you doing that . . . 'Here am I lying down on the ground. Do us a favour and tramp over us.'

BOB: I'm not doing that!

KATE: You look like it.

BOB: I'm not.

KATE: Sometimes, I think you're fantastic . . . I really do . . .

BOB: Ta . . .

KATE: Mostly when you're away from me.

BOB: Ta, again.

KATE: Just *said* that . . .

BOB: Bet you . . .

KATE: I hate people doing things just because they think I want them to do it. You don't understand? I was being like my father . . . And telling people . . . 'Do this . . . Do that . . . Don't do this . . . Don't do that . . .' I hate that. I do. It makes me mad.

BOB: Alright. Got the message.

KATE: It's all arranged. We're going over to look at this place your father's organised. Maybe help him. That's what you want us to do, isn't it? And don't bloody say 'I'm easy' or I'll kick you! I will!

BOB: I don't want you to do anything if it's going to kill you.

KATE: Don't flatter youself, son. If it was going to kill me, I wouldn't be doing it. None of us would be.

Words

BOB [*going forward*]: Come on. If we're going, let's get moving.

KATE [*taking his hand*]: Don't jump from the one side of the road to the other, Bob. If I don't want to trample on you, I don't want you trampling on me, either . . .

BOB: Tell you something, Kate. You don't know what you want us to do . . .

KATE [*closer to him*]: Now you're talking, Bob, son. That's more like it. The vibrations are getting better and better all the time. . . .

SCENE 7: *The shop.* MR CAMPBELL *is on a step-ladder, painting.* KATE *is near him, helping.* DAVID *is stripping paint from a door.* MARTIN *and* LOUISE *are taking some shelves down.* BOB *squats on the floor, cleaning brushes, but watching what's going on, tense.*

MR CAMPBELL: What I'm saying . . . If you get sick . . . You know . . . If it becomes a big drag. Forget it.

KATE: No. But it's great . . . This . . . We need somewhere like this. Don't we, Martin?

MR CAMPBELL: I'm just doing this because I fancy doing it. That's the whole point of it. It's one place you do what you want to do. No pressures one way or other.

DAVE: Serious . . . Do what you want to do . . . [*An arm round* KATE]

KATE: Dave. Drop, son! Drop!

DAVE: I'm just asking . . .

MARTIN: It just seems wrong to me. Not justice. Everybody working to pay that fifteen quid for my crankshaft . . .

LOUISE: For everybody to use . . .

MR CAMPBELL: If everybody uses the car . . .

KATE: God, I was *sick!* Up and down the stairs, stuffing in fish finger coupons . . .

MARTIN: You think we should have a drama group here? [*To* MR CAMPBELL]

MR CAMPBELL: Anything you want . . .

MARTIN: Yeah . . . It's 'OURS', isn't it . . . That's it! . . .

MR CAMPBELL: Call it what you want. I'm just throwing that to you.

KATE: After you've done it all up, you'll just fade out, will you?

MARTIN: If you want him to. That's the genie from Alladin's lamp. Just tell the man what you want . . .

MR CAMPBELL: Not the same scene, Martin. I want things, too . . .

LOUISE: It seems . . . You know . . . Sad, like . . . You doing all this . . . And then . . . Just going away . . . Doesn't it?

KATE: No, he likes doing it. That's what turns him on, isn't it? Building a better future for the next generation. That's great, isn't it, Martin?

MARTIN: I mean . . . All over the estate . . . Thousands of characters . . . Adults . . . Yeah . . .

Words

BOB [*unable to stand any more*]: I'm blowing.

KATE: That's the message, Bob. Do what you fancy here . . .

LOUISE: Bob . . . Where are you going?

MARTIN: What I'm saying . . . All over the estate . . . All these people . . . And a place like this turns up . . . You know . . . And if it wasn't for Bob's dad . . . See what I mean? . . .

DAVE: It would've been knocked down . . .

BOB: I'm going for a coffee. You coming, Kate?

KATE: I'm helping your father. No, I'm not coming.

MR CAMPBELL: Bein' knocked down next spring . . .

MARTIN: Next spring . . .

MR CAMPBELL: Could still be, if it doesn't work out.

BOB: I'm going to the café.

KATE: It's a thought, isn't it? [*To* MR CAMPBELL] If it hadn't been for you . . . [BOB *waits, looking at* KATE] Yeah. I heard you . . . Enjoy yourself.

MR CAMPBELL: I'll be here till about eleven, Bob. If you want a lift back . . .

BOB: Yeah . . . I'll see, Dad . . .

MARTIN: What you're on about, Mr Campbell, is what really *is* education, isn't it?

MR CAMPBELL: I'm on about freedom . . .

KATE: That's what Martin's saying . . .

MARTIN: This is what we need, kids, you know . . . Space to move . . . Without people pushing you . . . This way and that . . .

[MR CAMPBELL *thinks he's getting somewhere*]

MR CAMPBELL: That's it, Martin. You're getting the message. Loud and clear, man . . .

SCENE 8: BOB's *house* . . . MR CAMPBELL *is having a late cup of tea with his wife.*

MR CAMPBELL: I mean, at first you could see it was a big laugh . . .

MRS CAMPBELL: Bob went away early, did you say, Ralph?

MR CAMPBELL: Don't know why he went. There's a thing between him and Kate. Obviously bad vibrations between them that night . . .

MRS CAMPBELL: What did they say, like, Ralph? Laughing at you?

MR CAMPBELL: But you see, once they saw I wasn't trying to get them to do what I thought they should be doing . . .

MRS CAMPBELL: Is Kate attractive?

MR CAMPBELL: Great . . . and bright . . . They're all bright . . . They're a great crowd . . .

MRS CAMPBELL: And they're coming back . . . to help . . . are they?

MR CAMPBELL: If there's goodwill on both sides, and honesty, age doesn't mean anything, does it? I'm telling you . . . Once we got over the big laugh stage . . . We were really communicating . . . I'm telling you . . .

MRS CAMPBELL: You reckon Bob and Kate had had some kind of fight, do you?

MR CAMPBELL: I'm telling you, Sue. It proves everything I've said. We were really communicating . . .

SCENE 9: *The café.*

LOUISE: No. It's a shame for him . . .

MARTIN: Yeah. It's a shame, isn't it, Kate?

KATE: Poor soul. He's doing his best.

LOUISE: It is! It is!

DAVE: He's not a bad bloke. Long as he keeps his mouth shut . . .

KATE: It is, so it is. It's just a shame for the poor old soul . . .
[BOB *enters*]

KATE: Looking for talent, son?

DAVE: Want a chip, Bob?

KATE [*seeing now that* BOB *is in the grip of a strong emotion*]: What's the matter, Bob?

MARTIN: Hey, we had a great time tonight, man. Great scene . . .

BOB: Yeah. Big laugh, wasn't it?

MARTIN: Look. You wanted us to meet your old man, son . . .

BOB: Hilarious, wasn't it?

LOUISE: We finished the whole of the back room, Bob, after you'd left.

KATE: See. He's *your* father, Bob. You can't expect us to feel for him like you do.

DAVE: What's wrong with having a good laugh, Bob? Just a bit of a laugh . . .

KATE: *You* wanted us to come, didn't you?

MARTIN: I mean, honestly, Bob . . . Some of the things he comes out with . . .

BOB: What about your father? He comes out with all the great bloody things in the world, does he?

MARTIN: My father's hysterical, man. Nobody's saying he isn't. Kate's is incredible. You ever seen Kate's father?

KATE: He should be put in a museum, my father. Example of Early Scottish Man . . .

MARTIN: But they keep out of our lives, man. Don't want to start running around with the gang . . .

BOB: I'm on about *you*, I'm not on about my Dad. I'm on about you being rotten and mean. That's what I'm on about . . .
[*This is a new* BOB, *moved by great emotions. A* BOB *the group has never seen before.* KATE *is moved by him. There is something in him that she never suspected*]

Words 35

LOUISE: I told them, Bob, honest . . .

BOB: Alright . . . If it's a big laugh . . . Alright . . . Just walk out . . . Or tell him straight to his face. Tell him straight out to get stuffed . . .

KATE: Yeah, I know what you mean. It just came out, Bob.

BOB: I mean, that's *sick* that. Leading him on like that.

MARTIN: But if he can be led on like that he deserves it, doesn't he?

KATE: Yeah. It just kind of carried us away. It was rotten. You're right. It was . . .

DAVE: I mean, I think he's a good bloke, Bob. He is . . .

LOUISE: What do you want us to do, Bob? Just give up going there?

LOUISE: We promised we'd be back on Thursday night.

BOB: I won't be there. Tell you that!

LOUISE: Will we just stop going, Bob? You reckon that's the best thing?

KATE: No. That's mean. We should tell him, straight, like Bob says . . . What we think . . .

MARTIN: That he's sick . . . Like the rest of his generation.

KATE: If that's what you think, yeah.

BOB: And he isn't! He's not! It's *you* that's bloody sick! The way you went on, tonight . . .

LOUISE: We never really talked with him at all, did we? I mean, I tried . . . But the rest of you, you just messed around . . .

MARTIN: Tell you what. When we go back on Thursday . . .

BOB: Look, just leave him alone!

KATE: We promised we'd go back.

BOB: Just leave it like that, Kate. Just don't turn up.

KATE: You can't leave it like that. You want us to tell him he's sick . . . To get stuffed . . .

MARTIN: You want us to have this great talk with him . . .

DAVE: I had a good time, Bob, man. I like painting . . .
[BOB *is isolated.* KATE *moves to him*]

KATE [*taking his arm*]: Bob, you're right. We can be really rotten when we try . . .

BOB: You don't know anything about him . . .

KATE: See, it's not him that gets us. It's you, Bob. I just get mad when I see people, you know, not being able to stand on their own. It just gets me, Bob. Do you know what I mean? If you were two people, see . . . You going about the way you and him are friends . . . If you were two people, you and your father . . . That would be great. But the way you are just now, you just kind of get lost, in him . . .

BOB [*knocked by this, resisting it*]: Kate, I don't . . . I don't . . .
[*But even at the moment of denial clearly recognising something of the truth in her charge*] You don't know what happens inside of me. I'm telling you, it's nothing like that. It isn't.

SCENE 10: *The shop.* MR CAMPBELL *obviously shaken, but trying to fight back. From time to time, to cover his failure to cope, he attacks part of the wall with his paint brush. The group is round him,* DAVE *painting too, with* LOUISE.

MR CAMPBELL: Yeah. Well, that's alright. Great. That's what I said. If it's a drag . . . Blow . . .

KATE: See, we don't want this . . . [*Indicating shop*]

MR CAMPBELL: Yeah. I know. I've got the message, Kate . . . There's plenty of other kids'll be glad of it . . .

MARTIN: We're telling you why we don't want it, Mr Campbell. You're on about communicating . . .

KATE: A place like the café . . . It's there . . . If we're there or we're not . . . See what I mean? We can go, or not go . . .

MARTIN: This is lumber. We can't stand lumber . . .

LOUISE: We'd have to look after it, if it was ours, wouldn't we?

MR CAMPBELL: That's the whole idea . . .

DAVE: It's too organised, see.

MARTIN: Like a youth club, Mr Campbell.

MR CAMPBELL: I'm telling you . . . If it's not your scene . . . Alright . . .

KATE: I mean . . . It's great of you . . . Doing all this . . .

BOB: He *likes* doing it . . .

MR CAMPBELL: I'm not saying I understand what you are on about . . .

KATE: Same as me. I don't understand what you're on about.

BOB: He likes making things from nothing. That's his kick.

MR CAMPBELL: Now wait a minute, Kate. I'm not letting you away with that. We're back on the big high wall between the generations. That's not on, Kate . . .

MARTIN: You do up this place . . . Put money in it yourself . . . Graft . . . Then you hand it to the kids . . . And blow . . . That the idea?

MR CAMPBELL: What do you think, Martin? Should I stay on for the fun and games?

LOUISE: He just enjoys doing it.

MARTIN: That's all there is to it?

MR CAMPBELL: I mean, I just can't take that. I can't believe that. You get an offer of a place like this. No strings. Your own. And you turn it down. For what? I mean, let's start really talking. If you want to talk, let's really do some hard talking. What for?

KATE: You see, I can't see you just completely blowing from the scene, after you've done all this.

MR CAMPBELL: I don't know what I'm going to do . . .

MARTIN: What did you reckon the scene'd be, then? You'd drop in for a coffee with the kids? And a chat up?

MR CAMPBELL: I don't reckon anything . . .

KATE: You'd just go where your nose takes you . . .

MR CAMPBELL: I'm on about hard talking. I think it's important to you . . . That you face up to the real reasons for you turning down this place. I'm not worried about you turning it down. I'm telling you, I've got plenty of other kids ready to take it. The Tenants' Association's been on to me ever since I took the lease . . .

MARTIN: That's great then. If you're not worried . . .

KATE: What other reason? Honest, that's what we're telling you. That's our reason, and you just don't get it . . .

MR CAMPBELL: Yeah. That's wrong. I'm a bit knocked. It'd've been great if you had liked this place.

DAVE: It's too big a drag, Mr Campbell. Organising it . . . Have to organise coffee . . . And look after the place . . .

MR CAMPBELL: No, that's not it, Dave. [*Desperately trying to reach the kids*] I mean . . . It's great . . . You trying to be honest with me . . . That's fantastic. For that alone, that's worth anything. But if you want to go all out on honesty . . . I can see you're suspicious of me. You're bound to be. Doing all this . . . Giving you this place. I'm after something. I probably am . . . Yeah . . .

KATE: It doesn't matter, Mr Campbell, honest . . . [*Moved by his failure and desperation to communicate*]

MR CAMPBELL: Yeah. I haven't been a hundred per cent honest, even with myself. At the back of my mind I had this kind of dim idea of dropping in, maybe with a mate . . . Having a chat . . . God . . . All these divisions in the world! You just can't lie down and not try and do something about them . . . Can you?

LOUISE: It's us. Honest. You've just hit on a real screwed-up bunch. You could go out on the street, anytime, and get a

dozen, twenty kids that would grab this chance. It's just us. Isn't it, Bob?
[BOB *says nothing*]

MR CAMPBELL: Bob, that's not your scene. That soft, wet thinking . . . Is it, son? I mean . . . They're your friends. If you can't be honest with your friends, Bob . . .

KATE: See, you just can't get the message. You can't get the message. You can never get the message from us. It's two worlds. It is. It's speaking across two worlds. Our world and your world . . .

MR CAMPBELL: Look, I'm telling you, I'm not having that. It's nothing to do with age. Age means nothing. What's a 'kid'? The whole idea of a 'kid'? It means somebody alive. That's all it means. There's kids . . . and dead men . . . That's the only two worlds there is. You either stay a kid all your life, or you kind of die. That's kidding yourself, Kate. Soft thinking like that . . .
[*He looks at* BOB, *waiting for him to speak.* KATE *watches* BOB *too. The rest of the group look on.* BOB *looks at the group, then at his father*] They're your friends, Bob. You can't do anything about the soft thinking of your friends? . . .

BOB: I'm a bit lost, Dad. I don't know . . .

MR CAMPBELL: For God's sake, what are you on about, son? They're pushing out the old story about the generations not being able to speak together. For God's sake . . . What about us?
[*And now* BOB *moves to the first of what will be a series of rejections of his father*]

BOB: You see . . . You're *not* a kid, Dad . . . You're not a teenager . . . You're *not* twenty . . .

MR CAMPBELL: For God's sake . . .

BOB [*conscious that* KATE *is watching him*]: I mean, like cells in your body . . . And that, Dad . . . It's just a fact . . . It does mean something . . . Doesn't it . . . Your cells get older . . .

MR CAMPBELL: Bob. You're losing me. What are you trying to say, man? [*But already defeated . . . collapsing . . . utterly shaken*]

BOB: It's not right either, is it, Dad, you feeling the same as me? I mean . . . I'm saying . . . Even your body . . . Isn't it . . . Even if living through twice as many years as me . . . [*Somehow the rejection which* KATE *had been urging and willing on* BOB, *now that it has been brought about, alienates her from him*]

MR CAMPBELL: I don't understand you, son. You're losing me. I mean, that's just words . . . You're just throwing out words . . .

KATE [*going to his rescue*]: It's what Louise says. It's just us. You've just hit on a queer bunch of kids. You've no idea . . .

DAVE: I'm enjoying myself. I could paint all day, man . . .

BOB: It's facts, Dad . . . You know that. It's not just words . . . It's facts . . .

MARTIN: It's just the way things are, isn't it, Mr Campbell?

MR CAMPBELL: Look. Do us a favour. Just blow . . . And let's get on with my work . . . Will you? . . .

LOUISE: Honest . . . I enjoy helping . . .

KATE: We're bent. I'm telling you. Me worse than anybody . . .

DAVE: I'm starving. Fancy a bag of chips? Bring you a bag back when we pass, Mr Campbell?

BOB [*going*]: You working here late, Dad?

MR CAMPBELL: Yeah . . . You can get a lift back . . . If you want . . .

SCENE 11: *The street.* BOB *moves to* KATE's *side and tries to take her hand. But she rejects him.*

KATE: Hey, Martin. Lend us some chip money?

BOB: What's happening now, Kate?

MARTIN: If you spray it with DDT before you give us it back . . .

BOB [*totally lost*]: Hey, Kate!
[. . . *But* KATE's *eyes are on the roads . . . and the cars rushing past . . .*]
. . . Kate . . . Kate! . . .

THE END

Cabbages

GAIE HOUSTON

CAST

HEADMASTER
MISS FITT
MR HODGE
JOHN
RUTH
ANTHONY
NICHOLAS
ALICE
JANE
HUGH
NAOMI
BELINDA

All applications to perform this play, whether by amateurs or professionals, should be addressed to Hughes Massie Ltd, 69 Great Russell Street, London WC1

Cabbages

SCENE: *A classroom. A platform step-ladder stands with a small table to the left of it. There are two stacks of chairs, one on each side. A handbell tolls monotonously as the pupils arrive. Each bears on his or her back a paper marked with an IQ. Below that is written A, and below that C/D. Each wears a cabbage on the head.* JOHN's *cabbage is the smallest, and* ANTHONY's *the biggest.* JOHN *enters last, with his arms round* RUTH *and* NAOMI. *The* HEAD *arrives at the same moment, and glares until the three detach themselves and go to put their books away, as the other pupils have done.*

HEAD: A time and a place, John. And the place for that sort of thing is not in public. And the time for that sort of thing, as far as you're concerned, is about five years hence. Hear me?

JOHN: Yes, sir. [HEAD *mounts platform steps and sits*] Only Naomi felt sick. [*The bell has stopped. A marching tune, badly played on a tinny piano, begins. The pupils get into line and march round, ending in two ranks.* MISS FITT *enters and stands beside the step-ladder*]

RUTH [*to* NAOMI]: Are you all right?

ANTHONY: Silence!

HEAD: I am waiting.

NICHOLAS [*sings quietly*]: For a white Christmas.

ANTHONY: Who sang that? [*Pause*]

MISS FITT [*nervous*] You've forgotten your places again. [*The pupils sort themselves so that all the girls are left and the boys right*]

HEAD: Co-education is a privilege, and you're abusing it. [NAOMI *sways and* RUTH *leads her to the side to sit on a metal chair*] You're soft. [*He reads from some papers in his hand*] We lost yesterday's match by nine goals to two. [*Looks up*] We have not won a match this term. [*Hands a paper to* MISS FITT] Half of you seem to have lost all your healthy competitive spirit. So, to spur you on, Miss Fitt is going to write your aggression ratings on your backs. [*She begins to do so, with a wide felt pen*] And I may say that with few exceptions, the results are a disgrace to the school. You've got to learn to beat people. You've got to push and thrust in this world, to come top in life.

NICHOLAS: How long you going on, sir? Can we sit down?

HEAD: No you may not. Heads up. Backs straight. Alice, come out here. [*She does so*]

ALICE: O dear, me again.

HEAD: Alice, you have been allowed in this sixth form with only average brains. Now I find that you are also bottom of the form in aggression. I'm warning you. Now go back to your place.

ALICE: Do I have to be aggress . . .?

HEAD [*interrupting*]: Instantly! [*She jumps into line. The* HEAD *reads from another paper, in a rapid bored voice*] We have to thank last term's leavers for the gift of a gramophone. [*The pupils clap*] That'll do.

JANE: Where is it, please?

Cabbages

HEAD [*ignoring her*]: This is important. I shall be bringing the Chairman of the Education Committee round the school this morning. I want him to find mature attitudes and instant obedience from all of you.

HUGH: Jane spoke.

HEAD: Well?

JANE: No, it's nothing.

HUGH: She said 'Where's the record-player?'

HEAD: It will be produced when required.

HUGH: It was given to us.

HEAD: I'm warning you, Hugh. We've heard from you before. Now. Prayers. [*All except him kneel*] For what we are about to dish out, may you be truly grateful. Hocus pocus norum malorum.

ALL: Amen. [*The marching music begins. All stand as the* HEAD *and* MISS FITT *go out. The music stops and the pupils fetch metal chairs, which they arrange in a V. While this is happening,* RUTH *joins* ALICE *and* NAOMI]

ALICE: How do you feel now?

NAOMI: It's going off. I'm all right, thanks.

ALICE: It's the second time this week.

RUTH [*gently*]: Don't worry, Alice. John and I'll take care of her.

ALICE: Is there anything?

RUTH: Nothing we can't take care of if we help each other.

ALICE: John looks so pale lately. [MISS FITT *enters and claps her hands.* BELINDA *and* JANE *sit down. The others go on talking among themselves*]

RUTH: We'd better sit down.

ANTHONY: Come along, there. [*He sits.* MISS FITT *mounts the platform steps and sits*]

NAOMI: We'd better sit down.

MISS FITT: Please, everybody. I know you don't like it. But I have to teach you, and you have to do as you're told. It's the system. Now we'd better go over our pigeon-holing before the exams.

ANTHONY: O, must I, Miss Fitt?

MISS FITT: Well, I must say, Anthony, you do seem to have everything in its pigeon-hole already. You work alone, if you will. [*He turns his chair and sits facing away, sometimes reading, and sometimes listening to the class.* MISS FITT *reads examples from a book*] Now, how would you label a lady who kept behaving as if she was ill, but did not seem to have anything wrong with her? [NICHOLAS, HUGH *and* BELINDA *put their hands up*] Alice, can you answer this?

ALICE: She'd be . . . I suppose she'd be very unhappy.

MISS FITT: That's not what's written in the back of the book, dear. Hugh?

NICHOLAS: Hypochondriac.

ANTHONY: Neurotic.

HUGH: A typical bloody woman. [*Some laughter*]

MISS FITT: That's enough. Now. What would you call a

person you saw giving away his own money, and breaking someone else's gun?

NICHOLAS: A lunatic.

BELINDA: No, a revolutionary.

JOHN: I'd call him a saint.

ANTHONY: Yes, you would. But a man like that's a dangerous revolutionary.

NAOMI: I'd call him by his name whatever it was. I hate pigeon-holing.

MISS FITT: It's part of the curriculum.

HUGH: Catch him destroying my gun! An anarchist, that's what he'd be.

RUTH: A saint!

MISS FITT: O dear, O dear, you're thinking again, Ruth. Goodness knows this school has done its best to get you out of the habit. I'm afraid there's nothing for it. We'll have to revise our attitudes. Third form work. [JANE *turns her chair round*]

JANE: I needn't do that. All my attitudes have been absolutely rock-hard since I was about three. [*She ogles* ANTHONY *and moves her chair nearer his*]

MISS FITT: All of you. Now come along. And don't forget that we may be having a visitor. We'll start with an easy one. Which is better, serious music or jazz?

ALL: Serious music.

JOHN [*at the same time*]: Jazz.

MISS FITT: How does it feel to be British?

ALL: We're proud to be British.

BELINDA: But we look with peace and tolerance at the rest of the world.

NICHOLAS: As long as it stays where it is.

HUGH: No wogs here.

MISS FITT: No, Hugh, that is not in the answer.

HUGH: I knew that would annoy her.

MISS FITT: We'd better do some instant examples. Now, quickly. [*She holds up a card marked 'Advertising'. The class boos. In this and the following responses,* JOHN, RUTH *and* ALICE *are less eager than most of the class. She holds up* 'Christianity'. *They clap.* 'Democracy.' *They clap.* 'Money.' *They boo*] John, why aren't you joining in?

JOHN: I can't see why we boo at money.

MISS FITT: Would anyone like to tell him? [*All the class except* NAOMI, ALICE *and* RUTH *put their hands up*]

BELINDA: O I know. O please, Miss Fitt.

ANTHONY: It's third-form stuff.

MISS FITT: Jane, would you like to help John?

JANE: Money doesn't buy happiness.

BELINDA: Money's sordid.

JANE: Beauty cannot be bought.

MISS FITT: I must say, John, I am surprised that you should

Cabbages

question that attitude. I thought you were so nice and unworldly.

JOHN: I am growing up, Miss Fitt.

NICHOLAS [*aside*]: If in doubt, ask the girls.

MISS FITT: Let's get back to the book. It's so much clearer if we go by the book. I get a little panicky with all this questioning. [*She holds up a card marked 'Antiques'. They clap. 'Plastic flowers.' They boo. 'Wordsworth.' The response is mixed*] Now make your minds up.

HUGH: Wordsworth's OK. Everyone knows that.

BELINDA: No. He's OK for O-levels. But you have to laugh at him for A-levels. That's right, isn't it?

MISS FITT: I'll just look it up.

ANTHONY: That book's out of date. The new OK intellectuals say Wordsworth's an OK poet. So for the next ten years, that's what he is.

MISS FITT: Thank you, Anthony. [*The* HEAD *and* MR HODGE *enter*] Now. [*She holds up 'Beethoven'. They clap*] And a more advanced one. ['*Cannabis.' They boo.* ANTHONY *hisses*]

HEAD: Very good, Anthony. [*The class stands*] Carry on, carry on.

MISS FITT: Fetch chairs, someone. [ANTHONY *places two chairs and the visitors sit. The class turn their chairs round and put them in a diagonal and sit*]

HEAD: This is Mr Hodge. He is kindly taking an interest in you.

MR HODGE [*a heavy and slow-moving man*]: You're lucky. You're all very, very lucky.

ANTHONY [*standing*]: On behalf of the Sixth Form, I would like to welcome you to the school, sir. [*Sits*]

HODGE: Yes. Well. What you going to do for us, then?

JOHN: We could read our essays.

JANE: We could sing for you.

HODGE: Sing? No. Can't you girls show me some needlework or something?

BELINDA: We're too clever to do needlework. We learn Latin.

HODGE: Wonderful. I only wish I'd had your chances.

JANE: Alice does needlework.

HEAD: I'm sure Mr Hodge doesn't want to see Alice's needlework. [*Loud aside to* MR HODGE] Barely average IQ. Very poor background.

HODGE: Got any boxers among you boys, have we? Show us a bit of boxing?

JOHN: We don't box.

HUGH: Worse luck.

JOHN: The girls won't box, you see.

HODGE: Tch tch tch. Co-education for you.

JOHN: So we do drama. We could act a play for you.

HODGE: No thank you. I don't hold with that kind of unhealthy swaggering about.

ALICE: So what about our compositions?

HEAD: Stop talking. I know. Let's hear their compositions.

Cabbages

HODGE: Very nice.

MISS FITT: Quickly now. Fetch them out. [*The pupils fetch them and return to their places*]

HODGE [*while this is happening*]: Indoor toilets. Heated classrooms. They're very, very lucky.

HEAD: Just need a few corners knocked off. Just need kicking into shape. I can make something of this lot. Make them decent members of a safe society. Let's have yours first, then Anthony. [*To* HODGE] Head boy. My best lad. He once learned the whole of the North-Eastern railway time-table by heart. A wonderful brain.

HODGE: I'd been in the mines three years when I was his age. He's lucky.

MISS FITT [*nervous*]: I've not seen these essays myself, Headmaster.

HODGE: Eh, we'll not see the spelling mistakes if they read them aloud.

MISS FITT: The subject was 'What I Want to Do'.

JANE: My mother said . . .

HEAD: Silence. Come along, Anthony.

ANTHONY [*stands*]: I'm terribly sorry, sir.

HEAD: What about?

ANTHONY: I haven't done it.

HEAD: You haven't . . .? Haven't done it? Your set work?

JANE: My mother said . . .

HUGH [*interrupting*]: And my father said.

HEAD: Silence! Well, Anthony. All I can say is that it's a very good thing that it's you, Anthony. I'm sure you'll have a good reason. But if anyone else . . .

ANTHONY: I tried, sir. But we've never been given any notes on the subject.

HEAD [*stands*]: Has anyone else not done their essay? [*To* HODGE] They won't try this again, once I've finished with them. [*To class*] Come on, hands up. [*All the pupils except* JOHN, ALICE *and* RUTH *put their hands up*]

BELINDA: I did try, sir. But I don't know what I want to do. It's not in the exam syllabus.

HUGH: There isn't a book on it.

JANE: Miss Fitt said we'd got to think for ourselves. But she ought to know better.

ANTHONY: It wasn't a fair subject. You haven't taught us what we want.

HEAD [*furious*]: O yes we have! I've taught you it all. Play the game. Watch the clock. Strive to come top. Love your neighbour. Respect your elders. We've taught you it all.

HODGE: What about hearing from someone who did write something down, then?

HEAD: Subversive. The lot of you. I'll knock it out of you.

HODGE: What about this little girl, then?

MISS FITT: Alice.

HODGE: Come on, Alice.

Cabbages

ALICE [*stands*]: I don't know if . . . I'm only average, you see. And in aggression I'm bottom. I'm not much good.

HODGE: Let's hear what she's done with the educational opportunities that I, as the taxpayer, have provided for her.

MISS FITT: Don't mumble, Alice. No one can hurt you.

ALICE [*reads, sometimes stumbling*]: What I want to do. I want to know myself, because I am often sad, and I do not want to be sad. I want to know how to be happy. When I should be thinking of history or geometry, I often wonder if anyone will be there when I go home. Or I wonder if anyone will ever marry me. I want to make someone very safe and happy, because I am not safe and happy, and I do not like it.

HEAD: Repetitive.

MISS FITT: Go on, Alice.

ALICE: I want some children, and I want to know how to look after their bodies, and how to let them be happy so that they will not be lonely when they grow up.

HEAD: She uses short words because her spelling is so atrocious.

HODGE: Well, what's it matter? They only marry, as she says. No use in educating girls.

ALICE: When I really think about it, I find that I do not really care at all about trigonometry or 'Paradise Lost'. I want to find out why I get headaches, and why I can suddenly be happy for a minute without any reason. I want to understand about people so that I can help them.

HEAD: Well go on. Stand up straight. Keep reading.

ALICE: That's all, sir.

HEAD: All? That's all? [*He snatches the book from her*] Look at it! No date. No margin. No paragraphs. [*He throws the book on the floor*] You've let me down. This whole class is a disgrace to the school. I shall take Mr Hodge away. And after break I shall return and expect to see a proper essay tidily written in every single book. Understand? [*The class stands as the* HEAD *and* MR HODGE *leave*]

HODGE [*as he goes*]: That's what the youngsters of today really want. A bit of discipline. They don't know what they're protesting about, you know.

HEAD [*from door*]: And no copying! [*Exit. Pause*]

NAOMI: I'm sorry, ma'am. We let you down.

MISS FITT: I let you down. The subject wasn't going to help you with your exams. I'll leave you now to write it. [*She comes down the steps and crosses to the exit*] He'll punish you if you don't write what he wants to hear. You know that.

ANTHONY: Can't we do a précis instead? Or analysis?

MISS FITT: I would rather you tried to understand what you want. I never did. [*Exit.* JOHN *follows her*]

HUGH: Damnation! There's nowhere to crib it from. [ANTHONY *moves to chair to think.* ALICE *moves, and* RUTH *and* NAOMI *follow her. The others wander and group together, talking quietly*]

RUTH: Poor old Alice. Not your day.

NAOMI: I'm rotten at aggression too, it seems.

RUTH: I wish he'd asked for my essay. I'm lucky, it's so easy

Cabbages

for me. I've always wanted to be a builder, and build good houses people could enjoy.

NAOMI: He'd have sneered at that too. Girls aren't builders.

RUTH: This one is.

NAOMI: I wish I knew what I wanted. If this . . . It's as if I've been swept up in a system and pushed where I never meant to go.

RUTH: You're free. And we love you. [*Enter* JOHN *with a record-player which he places on the table and plugs in*]

JOHN: Look at this. Our present. It was on top of the lockers.

NICHOLAS: Music while you work. Only don't let anyone hear.

ANTHONY: I must protest!

ALICE: It can be think-music. Let's put the chairs away. [*They do so. Music starts.* RUTH *and* JOHN *take the cabbages off their heads, as if they find them uncomfortable. They dance gently with* NAOMI. ALICE *dances alone. The rest sit on the floor*]

JOHN: I want to play the guitar and sing, and live with you two. It's kind of a short essay. [*He grins*]

NAOMI: I wish I knew . . . [RUTH *takes* NAOMI's *cabbage off*] What are you doing? Goodness. My head's so light! [*She stops, then jumps up and down once or twice, excited*] It's all right. I know what I want, and it's easy! [*Crosses to* ALICE] Look, take it off, and then you can think. [*She helps* ALICE *with the cabbage. The music stops.* HUGH *stands and comes forward*]

HUGH: Well, I'll say I want to be a schoolmaster. That'll please him.

JOHN: You could be a good schoolmaster.

HUGH: Chuck my weight around. Tell them what the book says. [JOHN *approaches him and tries to take his cabbage off and they retire together, having difficulty*]

NICHOLAS: I want to be a professional footballer.

ANTHONY: A waste of a good intellect, kicking a football about.

HUGH: A waste of a good footballer, kicking ideas about.

ANTHONY: No future in football.

RUTH: Anthony has a future, but he doesn't know what to do with it.

NAOMI: Anthony only has a past. How can he have a future?

BELINDA: I want to be a hairdresser and a beauty queen. I can't be top-brain, so I'll work at being top beauty.

NAOMI: You're beautiful already.

BELINDA: Come off it.

NAOMI: Take that thing off your head, and you'll understand. [*They move aside as* HUGH, *without his cabbage, suddenly yells and rushes about*]

HUGH: It's fantastic! Hey, take them off! It's fantastic! Where's my book? What an essay! I do want to be a schoolmaster, but not his kind. I'll try to let a person grow out of every child.

ANTHONY: A child is an empty vessel who has to be filled with information.

JANE: People are dangerous animals who must be curbed by the rules of educated society.

NICHOLAS: That's why football's good. It gets rid of nasty tendencies.

JANE: And helps you to beat people. Beat them. Beat them. [*She rushes at* NICHOLAS *and they struggle*]

NICHOLAS: You're only a girl. I can beat a girl.

RUTH [*trying to separate them*]: Get those things off your heads before you hurt each other.

NICHOLAS: I want to hurt her. [*She pulls the cabbages off and they stop and stare at each other, shocked*] O no I don't. [*They hug*]

JANE: I don't want to beat you. [*Music starts. The people without cabbages dance in wide slow movements*] I mean, I want us both to do things very well, but I'd rather help you than compete with you.

ANTHONY: You won't get far in this world without competition.

BELINDA: The survival of the fittest. It's a law of nature.

JOHN: Take your cabbage off.

RUTH: Competition is a law of this society. Loving people is a law of nature.

NAOMI: She can't hear you. She's got a cabbage on. She can't know you. She can't know herself.

NICHOLAS [*picking up a paper from the table*]: Look at that!

ANTHONY: Love is sentimental nonsense. It's just a comforter for failures. [*He indicates his back*] But some of us have power and success.

NICHOLAS: Turn round so that I can write your score on you.

ALICE: O please, no more scores.

JANE: But this is a nice one. It's our C/D ratings.

ANTHONY: It's a fact of life, that some of us are better than others. Am I top?

NICHOLAS: No, you're bottom. Bottom of the class.

BELINDA: Then it's me. I'm top, aren't I? [*He writes on her*]

JANE: Take your cabbage off and look.

BELINDA: All right. [*She pulls it off eagerly, but with difficulty*] O no.

JANE: Isn't it strange? It doesn't matter any more.

BELINDA [*to* ANTHONY]: There is a kind of success for every one of us. [NICHOLAS *writes a score on everyone's back*] We're all different, not better or worse. Don't be frightened of me. I'm not an enemy.

ANTHONY [*shaking his finger at her angrily*]: Now look here! You've got to be frightened of me. And stop that music and do as I tell you.

BELINDA: I'm going to do what *I* tell me, because I am quite wise about what I need to do.

NICHOLAS: Alice is top.

ANTHONY: No! She can't be. I'm top, I must be! It's very important to me, whatever it is, this C/D.

Cabbages

JANE: Compassion and delight. It's our capacity for compassion and delight.

JOHN: And the Head never bothered to tell us.

NAOMI [*to* ALICE]: There, love, you're top.

ALICE: No. Haven't you noticed? No one's bottom, and no one's top. We all add up the same.

BELINDA: No one better. No one worse. All just different.

ALL THE GIRLS [*linking arms and swaying. If possible, singing or chanting cheerfully*]: No one better. No one worse.

JOHN [*from the platform, costermonger style*]: Big ones, small ones, fat ones, thin ones! Every one a winner! They're lovely!

ALL [*surrounding* ANTHONY]: No one better. No one worse. All just different.

ANTHONY [*in torment*]: Stop getting at me. I can't think. [MISS FITT *enters*]

HUGH: Try feeling, then.

ANTHONY: I can't think. [*He pushes through the circle and joins* MISS FITT]

MISS FITT: If you take that off your head, perhaps you'll be able to.

ANTHONY: But what about you, ma'am?

MISS FITT: It's been on too long. But yours. [*He bends his head towards her and she tugs at the cabbage. He screams in pain and retreats. The others are dancing in two lines as they listen to what is happening*]

ANTHONY: No, leave me. I've got to keep it or I'll be lost. I know I'll be lost.

RUTH: We're not lost, Anthony.

ANTHONY: I've got more than ever you had.

NICHOLAS: Just take it off. Come on in, the water's warm.

ANTHONY: No.

HUGH: I'll help you.

MISS FITT: No. It's stuck on so hard, I think he must get it off by himself. He's too frightened to let us help him yet.

ANTHONY: Of course I'm not frightened.

JOHN: I'll try to tell you what it's like to be free. [*Coming forward*] We're settled back in ourselves. That's it. We're fully ourselves—not working against each other any more. I mean we're free to feel love.

ANTHONY: Love! [*Pushes past* JOHN *to* MISS FITT] Naomi's having a baby. Did you know that? [*Pause*]

MISS FITT: I was afraid of it. I wouldn't ask.

RUTH: It isn't true.

ANTHONY: She fainted yesterday. I'm not stupid, you know.

NAOMI: My heart's damaged. I can never have babies. The doctor told me on Friday.

JOHN: So she's going to live with Ruth and me and we'll, well, we'll have babies she can share. [RUTH *has brought* NAOMI *forward to stand between her and* JOHN]

MISS FITT: Poor Naomi. But it's not practical, John. People won't accept you if you live like that.

HUGH: I'll accept you, mate.

ANTHONY: Where's the guarantee that you won't be in the way?

NAOMI: There's no guarantee.

ANTHONY: If you aren't normal . . .

ALICE: Not better, not worse. Just different.

MISS FITT: But money, John. Who's going to pay for this strange household?

OHN: I'm working as a waiter three nights a week now.

RUTH: I work in a shop every Saturday. Saving for a flat.

NAOMI: I haven't felt so well. I'm only studying. But I'll pass all my exams. You said.

JOHN: We're not made of dreams, you know, Miss Fitt. We can live, if you'll just trust us.

MISS FITT: You're braver than ever I could be.

NAOMI [*pointing at her cabbage*]: If you took that off you'd find your courage.

RUTH: And you, Anthony. Join us. We're full of living, and you can be, too.

NICHOLAS: You're clever now. If you took that thing off your head you'd be a genius.

ANTHONY [*frightened*]: How do I know? [*To* MISS FITT] I came bottom in this C/D thing.

MISS FITT: But top in aggression.

ANTHONY: Is that best? I'm getting confused. I am frightened.

BELINDA: We are all here if you want us.

JOHN: Let him be. He may turn dangerous. He won't mean to. But he's got such a lot to react against, once he does begin to understand. [*All except* ANTHONY *and* MISS FITT *return to dancing, this time in twos and threes*]

ANTHONY: I won't lose my respectability?

MISS FITT: I'll always respect you.

ANTHONY: My principles?

MISS FITT: I don't know. [*With pain and effort* ANTHONY *pulls the cabbage off his head. He gropes as if blind*]

ANTHONY: Where've I gone? There's nothing to protect me. No conventions to lean against. No superiority to fend you all off with. It's all colours! It's blinding. [ALICE *moves towards him.* JOHN *restrains her, shaking his head*]

JOHN: Dance with us, little Alice. [*With sudden courage,* MISS FITT *pulls the cabbage off her head*] And you, Miss Fitt.

MISS FITT: Oh please. May I learn? [*The music changes to a loud joyful beat.* MISS FITT *and, after a moment,* ANTHONY, *join the group. They dance as a team, but without losing their own characters. At the climax of the music they are in a circle with all their hands joined and raised in the middle. The music cuts. They stop whirling and laugh and gasp and lean on each other, then stiffen as they see the* HEAD *enter. The group retreats as he moves to the platform and climbs up*]

HEAD [*grim*]: I've come to hear your essays.

Cabbages

MISS FITT: They've been thinking about them, Headmaster. Really they have.

HEAD: That [*pointing to the record-player*] is confiscated. Take it out! [*No move*] Take it out! Who brought it in here?

JOHN: I brought it in here.

HEAD: I'll make an example of you in front of the whole school.

NICHOLAS [*cheeky. With exaggerated mime-gestures to illustrate his words, he moves round*]: In so far as anything belongs to anybody, that record-player belongs to us.

HEAD: You're using it in my time.

RUTH [*also moving and miming, but cheerful*]: In so far as anything belongs to anybody [*slow menacing music starts quietly*], this time belongs to us too. It's the time of our lives. And that's what we want. To have the time of our lives. [*She puts her hands above her head, as if to dance*]

HEAD: Stop that. [*She freezes*] Do as I say. Put your arms down. [*All raise their arms*] I'll knock this out of you. I'll get you.

ALL [*all change position so they are pointing at him with one arm outstretched. They take a step forward in unison*]: I'll get you.

HEAD: I'll teach you! Stop it. I'll teach you! [ALICE, JOHN, NAOMI *and* HUGH *separate. The rest in slow motion change arms, and step forward again in unison*]

JOHN: What did you ever teach us, in all our years here?

HUGH: He cheated us! He taught us nothing.

ALICE: Not about our bodies.

C

HUGH: Not about our minds.

NAOMI: Not about our happiness.

HEAD: Algebra. Geometry. Latin. History.

NAOMI: He didn't even teach us to look after babies.

JOHN: Or how to make love.

HUGH: Or how the Government works, or what the laws are that we must live by.

ALICE: Or who we are, or what we want. [*The pupils who have not been speaking move closer in menacing slow motion to the* HEAD]

ANTHONY [*on the bottom step of the platform ladder*]: You've taken us away from ourselves. Old devil!

MISS FITT [*turning and coming quickly to the group*]: I can't control people. You must. He'll do something bad.

HEAD [*in panic*]: Top in aggression. You're my best lad. I made you.

ANTHONY: You made a killer of me. [*In the slow motion group each brings his right arm back above his head, as if about to strike. In* ANTHONY's *hand a flick-knife springs open. Everyone freezes for a count of four as the music stops. Then* NAOMI *reassures* MISS FITT. JOHN *crosses confidently to* ANTHONY *and the pupils round him drop their arms*]

JOHN [*touching* ANTHONY *lightly*]: If you kill him, you start to kill you. Violence [*he draws a wheel with his hand*] goes in circles.

HEAD: You seem to forget who you're dealing with. I'm the authority here. You're in my power. And I shall probably

Cabbages 67

call the police. [*He tries to get down the steps. Nobody makes way for him*] I can't help it. You've brought it on yourselves.

ANTHONY: He's dangerous, John. I've got to kill him, to set us free.

HEAD: I am not dangerous.

RUTH: Let him speak. [*The* HEAD *remounts the platform*]

HEAD: You are my children. I am trying to prepare you for a cruel, competitive world. A world of suffering and struggle and disappointment and failure.

BELINDA: That's your world that you're describing. We don't want to be fitted for it.

HUGH: We know ourselves, and we know that we are not competitive and cruel.

HEAD: You are being cruel to me now.

MISS FITT: They don't want to be. But you menace and distort them. [NICHOLAS *starts the record-player, with dancing music*]

NICHOLAS: Will you dance with me, Miss Fitt? It's not a competititon.

MISS FITT: I'd be delighted.

JANE: Let's dance together. [*All the pupils dance in varying groups and pairs*]

BELINDA: Poor old Headmaster. [*She indicates him, standing alone on the platform steps*]

ANTHONY: He could join us if he tried. Miss Fitt did. I did.

HUGH: Someone ought to dance with him.

JANE: Yuk.

BELINDA: Might catch a nasty dose of aggression off him.

ALICE [*to* HEAD]: Will you dance with me?

HEAD: Thank you. [*He comes down and starts an earnest out-of-rhythm foxtrot with her*]

ALICE [*to audience*]: I came top in compassion, you see. [*In ones and pairs, the others begin to gather their belongings and leave, hand in hand and laughing. The* HEAD *watches his feet and dances as best he can.*] Poor old thing. He can't help it. Just brainwashed from birth.

HUGH [*standing with* RUTH, NAOMI *and* JOHN *at exit*]: We're waiting for you. [*They stretch their hands to her and she goes out with them, entwined. The* HEAD *looks up and finds that he is deserted*]

HEAD: I still want those compositions, you know. I'm in charge. [*Shouting after them*] I said I'm in charge! Do you hear me!

[*But there is no reply*]

THE END

The Singing Door

DORIS LESSING

CAST

CHAIRMAN
FIFTH PRECEPT
FOURTH PRECEPT
SECRETARY
GUARDIAN OF THE DOOR
DELEGATES
TWO DISSIDENT DELEGATES
ATTENDANTS
GUARDS
FIRST LOW-LEVELLER
SECOND LOW-LEVELLER
THIRD LOW-LEVELLER
FOURTH LOW-LEVELLER
TWO MEDICAL ASSISTANTS
DOCTOR
ASSISTANT TO GUARDIAN OF THE DOOR
A GROUP OF PEOPLE FROM VARIOUS LEVELS
TWO LATE-COMERS
ASSISTANTS AND HELPERS AT THE ALTAR
TECHNICIAN

All applications to perform this play, whether by amateurs or professionals, should be addressed to Jonathan Clowes Ltd, 20 New Cavendish Street, London W1

The Singing Door

SCENE: *Is this a cave? If so, it is a cave into which has been fitted technical equipment. Perhaps it is an underground shelter for time of war? At any rate, this place combines a rawness of earth and rock with advanced gadgetry. This last is piled up at centre back in a way which suggests an altar or a sacred place: computer, radio receiving apparatus, television set, electronic devices—any or all of these. None of these things is working. In the middle of this arrangement is set, in the place of honour, an unattached wooden door. Every item is much garlanded and decorated, but the flowers and greenery are artificial. The altar's* ATTENDANTS *are wearing technicians' uniforms. They are in attitudes of worship, telling beads, muttering mantras, and so on.*

At left is a rough rocky exit into the deeper levels of this underground place.

At right is a large door, much more than man-size. It has a look of complicated and manifold function, and seems as if it might be organic, for it is hard to see how the thing is fastened into the rock. There is no jamb, lintel or frame. It seems more as if all that part of the rocky wall is, simply, door. And while it might be of brass, or bronze, or perhaps gold—any metal that by age comes to soften and glisten so that it coaxes and beguiles the eye—it might equally be made of some modern substance, glass, or plastic, or sound waves made visible. A faint humming sound can be heard, but it is more reasonable to assume that such a noise must come from the machines, even though these look dead—just as the eye is first drawn to them, in their central position, and not immediately to the great door, perhaps just because of its size and equivocal substance. Yet, once seen, the great door dominates, although, in contrast to the altar of technical objects, it looks neglected or ignored. The steps leading to it are undecorated.

At right front is a large round table with chairs set round it, glasses of water, scribbling blocks—the paraphernalia of a modern conference. One is in progress. On the breast of each DELEGATE *is a large badge with his or her status on it. They have no names. Each wears some sort of uniform, or stiff, formal clothing. The* DOCTOR *is dressed like a surgeon in an operating theatre. The* GUARDIAN OF THE DOOR *wears overalls like a mechanic, but he has religious and national symbols pinned or draped on him.*

There are ATTENDANTS *at the exit, left, and* GUARDS *behind the chairs of the* CHAIRMAN *and the* GUARDIAN OF THE DOOR.

CHAIRMAN: And that brings us to the end of our agenda. Thank you, all officers. Thank you, delegates.

[*People are already beginning to get up, but*]

FIFTH PRECEPT: Excuse me, not quite the end.

[CHAIRMAN *leafs to the end of his agenda, looks enquiringly at* FIFTH PRECEPT, *then laughs. So do some of the others*]

FIFTH PRECEPT: I wasn't joking, sir.

[*They sit down again, but they still smile as if at an old joke*]

CHAIRMAN: Fifth Precept, we have been in continuous session for nearly a week.

FOURTH PRECEPT: Or for several hundred years.

CHAIRMAN: Quite, quite. Fourth Precept, I do not think this is

The Singing Door

the right time for . . . it makes me nervous when anyone even jokes about time, measurements of time—that sort of thing, when it takes so little to start the bickering and disagreement off again. All very sincere people, very sincere, the historians and time-keepers, but . . .

FOURTH PRECEPT: I wasn't joking either, sir.

FIFTH PRECEPT: We would like to have the last item, Item 99, discussed and voted on.

FOURTH PRECEPT: Yes.

CHAIRMAN: When was the last time Item 99 was discussed, Secretary?

SECRETARY [*leafing through minutes*]: Just a moment. It's been so long that . . .

CHAIRMAN: Oh never mind.

FIFTH PRECEPT: It was fifteen years ago.

SECRETARY: Yes. That's right.

FIFTH PRECEPT: Which was when the problem arose last time.

GUARDIAN OF THE DOOR: There was a great deal of trouble. We had a lot of trouble, I remember.

CHAIRMAN: So I submit it can wait until tomorrow.

GUARDIAN: Or even next week.

[*The* DELEGATES *laugh*]

FIFTH PRECEPT: No. It must be now.

CHAIRMAN: Forgive me, Fifth Precept, but are you feeling well? We are all of us pretty tired, and it is quite understandable . . .

FIFTH PRECEPT: Quite well, thank you. [*He stands up*] Exalted Chairman! Guardian of the Door! Fellow Precepts! Delegates! Secretaries! . . . and so on and so on and so on. If you actually take the trouble to look at the wording of the last item, Item 99 [*Some members hurriedly do so*], you'll see that it reads: 'In view of the urgency, it is decided that full mobilisation is called at once. The Door is expected to open at hour zero.' Very shortly, in fact. [*There is general discreet amusement*] A great many people are expecting it.

CHAIRMAN: You know quite well that some nut is always announcing the Opening of that Door.

SECRETARY: Which is why we have Item 99 permanently on the Agenda, to take care of it.

FIFTH PRECEPT: Yet we all believe that the Door will open some time. And that when it does we can leave this place.

DELEGATE: Of course we do.

DELEGATE: Of course.

CHAIRMAN: If there had been any indication from Centre [*He indicates the machines and their worshippers*] we would have been told.

FIFTH PRECEPT: Our life in this place is entirely organised around our expectation of this Opening. If we didn't believe that we would one day escape, that our people would one day reach the open air and the light-of-day . . .

DELEGATE: Whatever they may be!

FIFTH PRECEPT: . . . the light-of-day, it would not be possible to sustain life here.

DELEGATE: Hear, hear.

The Singing Door

SECRETARY: Article 17 of our Declaration of Faith. Very fine, but is a conference the right place for this sort of thing?

GUARDIAN: As First Guardian of the Door I must protest against the tone of our Secretary.

SECRETARY: Sorry, Guardian. [*As* GUARDIAN *does not relent, he recites*] I offer my thoughts, being and intentions in total apology for blasphemy. Unintentional blasphemy atonable for by simple-form apology.

GUARDIAN: Simple-form apology accepted with warning.

CHAIRMAN: Can we get on? I adjourn the conference until tomorrow.

FIFTH PRECEPT: I object.

CHAIRMAN: Overruled.

FIFTH PRECEPT: According to Rule 954 I have the right to insist.

CHAIRMAN: Wait a minute. [*He and* SECRETARY *consult the rules*] I see. Very well then—you're ill. You must be. I've never been more upset to see a colleague of mine fall under the weight of duty. You'd better take leave. From this evening.

FOURTH PRECEPT: And must I join him?

CHAIRMAN: Oh no, it's too much . . . when two of this, the highest body of our people, fall victim to . . . yes, both of you, take a month's leave.

A DELEGATE WHO HAS NOT YET SPOKEN: And me too?

[FOURTH *and* FIFTH PRECEPTS *look at him in surprise, then at each other*]

ANOTHER DELEGATE: And me?

[FOURTH *and* FIFTH PRECEPTS *and the last speaker are surprised*]

CHAIRMAN: Four of you. I see. I don't know why I didn't see it before—this is obviously yet another attempt from the Low-Levellers to take over. Obviously.

[FOURTH *and* FIFTH PRECEPTS *and their two supporters laugh*]

FIFTH PRECEPT: As soon as the Low-Levellers come into it, that's the end of all reason.

CHAIRMAN: We all know that you represent the Low-Levellers, that you work for their interests, that you improve their conditions—and of course, we all honour you for it.

FIFTH PRECEPT: Really? I hadn't noticed it.

CHAIRMAN: Of course, without reformers there's no progress. But. The Low-Levellers always overstep the mark sooner or later. We know that too, and expect it.

FOURTH PRECEPT: And make provision for it by putting under the last item of every agenda their requests, reasonable or otherwise, about the Door.

CHAIRMAN: I am glad you can admit they are sometimes unreasonable.

FIFTH PRECEPT: I and Fourth Precept assure you that this has nothing to do with the Low-Levellers.

THE TWO DELEGATES WHO SUPPORT THEM: Nothing. Nothing at all.

A DELEGATE: May we then ask who inspired your conviction that the Door is about to open?

The Singing Door

FIFTH PRECEPT: For one thing, look at it.

[*They turn to look at the door in the middle of the stack of machinery*]

CHAIRMAN: Well?

A DELEGATE: It has never changed since I first saw it.

ANOTHER: My father served on this committee and he said it never altered in his lifetime.

FIFTH PRECEPT: Not that Door. The other one.

A DELEGATE: What Door?

ANOTHER: What other Door?

CHAIRMAN: As you two are new on this committee, you may not know that certain deviant and of course unimportant sects have always maintained that the real Door is that one. [*He nods at the Door, right. The* GUARDIAN *coughs*] I apologise.

GUARDIAN: It is not your fault these heresies continue.

DELEGATE: Funny, I never even noticed it.

GUARDIAN: Which is not surprising.

FOURTH PRECEPT: It is easily overlooked.

FIFTH PRECEPT: Until you have seen it—but then some people find it hard to look at anything else.

ONE WHO STARES AT THE ALTAR: Why, it isn't even attached to anything. It doesn't lead anywhere.

ANOTHER: It isn't anything at all.

GUARDIAN [*on his feet and obviously about to launch into an oration*]: My children, in this unfortunate time, let us all take heart and . . .

CHAIRMAN: Quite so, oh quite so, Guardian, but perhaps I should deal with this? [GUARDIAN *seats himself again*] Secretary, have you file Number 7? [SECRETARY *hands over file 7*] Last week, our investigators found evidence of a new subversive cult and . . .

FIFTH PRECEPT: You mean, our spies.

CHAIRMAN: If you like. But there is unrest. Serious unrest.

[*There is noise beyond the left opening. One of the* ATTENDANTS *comes running to the conference table*]

ATTENDANT: Some of them insist on coming in.

CHAIRMAN: You have forgotten something, I think?

ATTENDANT: Second Hereditary Attendant to the Gate to the First Level. Some of them insist on coming in.

CHAIRMAN: They can wait until tomorrow.

[*A second* ATTENDANT *runs over*]

THIS ATTENDANT: First Hereditary Attendant. They've got hand-grenades.

CHAIRMAN: I knew it. [*To a* GUARD] Arrest the Fourth and Fifth Precepts.

FIFTH PRECEPT: You haven't the authority.

CHAIRMAN: Haven't I!

SECRETARY: Precepts cannot be arrested without a week's full notice and then only after having posted . . .

The Singing Door

CHAIRMAN: Oh never mind. Doctor—Precept Doctor?

[DOCTOR *stands up*]

FIFTH PRECEPT: There's no appeal against that.

CHAIRMAN: No.

[*The* DOCTOR *takes* FOURTH *and* FIFTH PRECEPTS *over to right. He claps his hands. Two white-overalled* MEDICAL ASSISTANTS *come running from left with a rolled stretcher, bottles of pills, a syringe. All the* DELEGATES *are watching these arrangements. The two who supported* FOURTH *and* FIFTH PRECEPTS *rise and go over and join them*]

SECRETARY: Heroic!

CHAIRMAN: But futile.

FIRST HEREDITARY ATTENDANT: Exalted Chairman, they give us five minutes. They have the pins out of their grenades.

CHAIRMAN: We bow to force. Let them in.

[*Two* LOW-LEVELLERS *come in. They are dressed in sweaters and jeans, have long hair, carry grenades*]

CHAIRMAN: Who are you?

FIRST LOW-LEVELLER: That doesn't matter.

CHAIRMAN: We must know with whom we are dealing.

SECOND LOW-LEVELLER: We are from Level 56.

[*Murmurs of shock and surprise from the* DELEGATES]

FIRST LOW-LEVELLER: Yes, this is the first time any one of you have set eyes on Level 56-ers, isn't it?

CHAIRMAN: Your status?

SECOND LOW-LEVELLER: Oh tell them, if it keeps them happy.

FIRST LOW-LEVELLER: Officer First Class, Second Subsidiary Grade.

SECOND LOW-LEVELLER: Officer First Class, Second Subsidiary Grade.

FIRST LOW-LEVELLER: *Elected* officers.

CHAIRMAN: Impossible.

SECRETARY: Sir, there was that revolution last month in the Intermediate City.

CHAIRMAN [*affable*]: Ah, so you are the leaders of the successful coup in the Intermediate City?

FIRST LOW-LEVELLER: You can put it like that if you can't understand it any other way.

[*From the left comes a muffled shout*]

We have no leaders!

[*Some more* LOW-LEVELLERS *come into view, trying to force their way past the* ATTENDANTS.
FIRST *and* SECOND LOW-LEVELLERS *turn so that they are able simultaneously to keep the* DELEGATES *controlled with their hand-grenades, and watch the entrance left.*
THIRD *and* FOURTH LOW-LEVELLERS *burst in, with rifles. They are wearing a lot of leather, and have short hair*]

THIRD LOW-LEVELLER: It is no use trying to keep us out.

CHAIRMAN: Very well, I suppose there is nothing for it. I declare the conference reopened, for discussion on Item 99. Will you please all be seated?

The Singing Door

FOURTH LOW-LEVELLER: A committee! Would you believe it!

FIRST LOW-LEVELLER: We might have known it.

SECOND LOW-LEVELLER: I'm not wasting my time talking.

THIRD LOW-LEVELLER: I'll give you exactly three minutes.

FOURTH LOW-LEVELLER: And don't imagine we wouldn't use them.

CHAIRMAN: You don't want to discuss Item 99?

FIRST LOW-LEVELLER: We don't want to *discuss* anything.

GUARDIAN: What do you want then?

SECOND LOW-LEVELLER: To have full representation in the celebrations tomorrow.

THIRD LOW-LEVELLER: The Ceremony of the Garlanding of the Door.

CHAIRMAN: I'd almost forgotten about that. We have a rehearsal in a few minutes, haven't we?

GUARDIAN: Do you mind repeating that? You have forced your way in here because you want representation for Level 56 in the Garlanding Ceremony?

THIRD LOW-LEVELLER: Not only 56. All the levels beyond that too.

CHAIRMAN: But it's not physically possible to have representatives from all the hundred levels. That was why it was arranged by the First Ones that the levels from 1 to 50 should represent 50 to 100.

GUARDIAN: But after all, we haven't been faced with fifty extra people, only four.

FOURTH LOW-LEVELLER: It was never anything but a disgustingly unfair arrangement.

CHAIRMAN: Yet I see that you and your friend are happy to represent all the levels beyond 56. Isn't that so?

FIFTH PRECEPT: Exalted Chairman, may I remind you that we are placed here because you decided that we were part of this—demand?

A DELEGATE: Conspiracy!

ANOTHER DELEGATE: Undemocratic and violent overthrow of Constitutional Government!

CHAIRMAN: Well well, I don't know. Perhaps we of the upper levels have got a bit stuffy. I see no reason at all why Level 56 shouldn't be represented at the ceremony. And they may start by joining us in the rehearsal.

FIFTH PRECEPT: Just a minute. We were arrested because you believed us to be party to this demand, or conspiracy.

CHAIRMAN: You haven't been arrested.

FIFTH PRECEPT: Thank you.

[*He and the other three attempt to leave the group of* DOCTOR *and* MEDICAL ATTENDANTS, *but they are forcibly restrained*]

FOURTH PRECEPT: We are being wrongfully held. On two counts. One, we knew nothing about this conspiracy. Two, it is now apparently not considered a conspiracy.

CHAIRMAN: Precept Doctor, we have not yet had your report.

FOURTH PRECEPT: There is no need of any report. We are all perfectly well.

The Singing Door

DOCTOR: Of course this is only a provisional diagnosis, but in my opinion these patients are not fit to leave medical care.

FIFTH PRECEPT: We aren't patients.

DOCTOR: There. Come now. Relax. Take these pills. You are getting over-excited.

[*The two* PRECEPTS, *then the other two refuse the pills, as the* DOCTOR *threatens force*]

FIRST LOW-LEVELLER: What's wrong with them? Who are they?

CHAIRMAN: You mean you don't even know your champions? Those are the famous Fighting Precepts.

FIRST LOW-LEVELLER: Champions!

SECOND LOW-LEVELLER: I think I've seen their pictures.

THIRD LOW-LEVELLER: Liberals!

FOURTH LOW-LEVELLER: Vacillating temporisers!

FIRST LOW-LEVELLER: Compromising timeservers!

CHAIRMAN: Well, well. And these are the people you have been fighting for.

FIRST LOW-LEVELLER: But what's wrong with them?

FIFTH PRECEPT: We are under medical care because we insist on discussing Item 99. Tonight.

SECOND LOW-LEVELLER: Never heard of it.

FIFTH PRECEPT: The Door is going to open. It is going to open.

THIRD LOW-LEVELLER: Oh I see, they're nuts.

GUARDIAN: I do so hope that you young people are not unbelievers. For while I deprecate the emotional extravagance and wrongheadedness of officers like the Fourth and Fifth Precepts, I find it in my heart to prefer that to total nullity.

FIFTH PRECEPT: But it is going to open.

FIRST LOW-LEVELLER: Well, of course it is. Who said it wasn't?

SECOND LOW-LEVELLER: We've all been taught that in school.

THIRD LOW-LEVELLER: Whether we liked it or not.

FOURTH LOW-LEVELLER: I didn't mind the Door lessons. I love those old myths.

GUARDIAN: Myths, indeed! Then why do you want to take part in the Door Ceremony?

FOURTH LOW-LEVELLER: It is a question of political equity.

FIRST LOW-LEVELLER: Justice.

SECOND LOW-LEVELLER: Liberty.

THIRD LOW-LEVELLER: Freedom.

FIFTH PRECEPT: But it will open. The Door will open.

[*Shouting*] Let me go. I must be free to tell everybody. I must . . .

[*The* MEDICAL ATTENDANTS *grab him. The* DOCTOR *deftly injects him, an* ATTENDANT *crams pills into his mouth. He passes out, and is laid on the stretcher. The* DOCTOR *tries to inject the* FOURTH PRECEPT, *who mimes submission, contrition, humility. As this is seen to work, the* DOCTOR *becoming avuncular and bland, the other two copy the* FOURTH PRECEPT.

The Singing Door

Meanwhile FOURTH PRECEPT *goes forward a little way to examine the big Door. He is joined by the two who have now mollified the* DOCTOR. *Do we imagine it, or is this Door brighter than it was?*]

THIRD LOW-LEVELLER: There have been a lot of pretty funny rumours down in the Levels recently.

CHAIRMAN: I would hardly describe a revolution as a rumour.

FIRST LOW-LEVELLER: No, about the Door. Rumours about the Door.

SECOND LOW-LEVELLER: More than rumours. There's a new sect.

THIRD LOW-LEVELLER: The main one calls itself 'The Door Will Open Soon' Society.

GUARDIAN: Indeed?

SECOND LOW-LEVELLER: There's been some rioting.

GUARDIAN: Very true. I had them arrested and imprisoned.

THIRD LOW-LEVELLER: I heard some escaped. We thought they might be here.

[FIRST *and* SECOND LOW-LEVELLERS *look suspiciously at* THIRD *and* FOURTH LOW-LEVELLERS, *while moving closer together.* THIRD *and* FOURTH *do the same. At the same moment, the two couples aim their grenades and their rifles at each other*]

CHAIRMAN: Now, now. There's no need for that.

[*A fresh commotion outside left exit.* ATTENDANT *comes running over*]

ATTENDANT: Second Hereditary Attendant of the Gate to the . . .

CHAIRMAN: Yes, yes, yes, yes, yes.

ATTENDANT: There's another lot.

CHAIRMAN: Then let them in, by all means.

[*This time there is a group of varying ages, and variously dressed. They are unarmed, and they walk quietly*]

CHAIRMAN: Delighted to see you all.

GUARDIAN: Do come in.

SECRETARY: You are more than welcome.

DELEGATES: Hear, hear. Yes. Of course. Welcome.

ONE OF THE GROUP: Oh, I'm so glad. We thought we might not believe it.

CHAIRMAN: No, no, we think every Level should be represented. Every one, mark you, including Levels 50 to 100. You will all be welcome at the Ceremony. And indeed, we were just about to start the rehearsal for tomorrow.

GUARDIAN: And it is time to start. Do join us.

[*He stands facing the pile of machinery, as if heading a procession. The* DELEGATES *and officers start forming behind him*]

ONE OF THE GROUP: But why does there have to be a Ceremony? Aren't we just going to walk right out?

[*This person, then others of the group, look at the Door propped up on the altar, look at each other, shake their heads,*

The Singing Door 87

then start looking around. One sees the big Door right, indicates it to the others. This group move over towards it]

CHAIRMAN: Doctor, you have some more patients.

FOURTH PRECEPT: I'm glad you made it. But be quiet. Don't argue. Don't fight.

[*This new group, the* FOURTH PRECEPT, *his two allies, are now close to the big Door. It is hard now to doubt that it is brighter. And surely the humming sound is louder*]

FIRST LOW-LEVELLER: I've never seen any of that lot before.

THIRD LOW-LEVELLER: I wonder what Level they are from?

ONE OF THE NEW GROUP: We come from all the Levels. Not just from one.

FOURTH LOW-LEVELLER: Are you from 'The Door Will Open Soon' Society?

ANOTHER OF THE NEW GROUP: From all the societies.

ANOTHER: Or from none.

GUARDIAN: Shouldn't we be getting on? Chairman?

CHAIRMAN: Of course. Assistant to the Guardian of the Door . . .

[*One of the* DELEGATES *whose function this is starts shepherding members of the Conference, and the* LOW-LEVELLERS, *into a neater line behind the* GUARDIAN. *He hands them garlands of plastic and paper flowers*]

GUARDIAN: I'll just run through my opening lines. [*As if delivering a sermon, but rather fast*] Many thousands of years ago, no one knows how many, a natural disaster or a war sealed us in this Under Place. We understand from the old records that a few survivors, known to us as The First People, laid the basis of this our society, excavating the First Level of the Under City. Water supplies were discovered and ensured, and the cultivation of mushrooms, our staple food, begun. The Sacred Machines were placed here, at the gate of the Outside, for it was revealed to the First People that it will be the Sacred Machines which will announce to the Door the moment it must open. . . . Et cetera and so on.

A DELEGATE: Lovely old stuff, isn't it?

ANOTHER: I've done this so often I could do it in my sleep.

ANOTHER: If the Door did actually open some of us would get the shock of our lives.

ANOTHER: We take it for granted there *is* something outside.

ANOTHER: Speak for yourself. I, for my part, am quite sure there is not.

ANOTHER: My attitude is that since we don't know, we should keep an open mind.

ANOTHER: Then why are you in this Ceremony at all? It is just hypocrisy.

CHAIRMAN: Nonsense, it is part of our ethic. Part of the fabric of our society.

DELEGATE: It does no harm and it may do some good.

SECRETARY: Refusing to take part in the Ceremony creates a disturbance. It is anti-social. It just draws attention to yourself, that's all.

The Singing Door

GUARDIAN: Your reasons for being here are not important. There are many paths to the Door. [*To his* ASSISTANT] The regalia?

ASSISTANT: Here. [*He hands* GUARDIAN *the regalia, and assists him—a plastic smock with silver lightning flashes, a mitre, a small transistor radio in one hand, a telephone in the other. The latter is a child's toy, in a bright colour*]

GUARDIAN: I think that's all. Assistant?

ASSISTANT: Lights. Lights. Turn down the lights.

[*A* TECHNICIAN *vainly clicks switches on the side of the computer*]

TECHNICIAN: Sorry, but they don't seem to work. I've turned off the usual number of lights but it is no darker.

FOURTH PRECEPT: Look at the Door.

A MEDICAL ATTENDANT: It's much brighter.

DOCTOR: It's an optical illusion.

[*But now there is no doubt that the Door is brighter*]

ONE OF THE NEW GROUP: It's getting brighter all the time.

GUARDIAN: Well, never mind. I'm sure the technicians will get everything right in time.

ANOTHER OF THE NEW GROUP: "Wait and watch for the sudden time,
The song that's bright,
The singing light.'

[ASSISTANT TO THE GUARDIAN *tries to push* FIRST *and* SECOND LOW-LEVELLERS *to the back of the procession. They resist. He tries with the* THIRD *and* FOURTH LOW-LEVELLERS]

FIRST LOW-LEVELLER: You don't seem to have got the point. Those days are over.

ASSISTANT: Everyone has to go where he is allocated.

FOURTH LOW-LEVELLER: No. Take your hands off.

CHAIRMAN: Move up here, behind me. We have got the point, I assure you.

[ASSISTANT *pushes* FIRST *and* SECOND LOW-LEVELLERS *up to the head of the procession behind* GUARDIAN]

THIRD LOW-LEVELLER: Very nice.

ASSISTANT: You can't all four be up at the front.

GUARDIAN: Of course they can. The youth are our most precious possession, the gold of our future. Let them come.

[ASSISTANT *pushes* THIRD *and* FOURTH *into the procession behind* FIRST *and* SECOND LOW-LEVELLERS]

THIRD LOW-LEVELLER: I'm sorry, but our status is just as relevant as their status.

FOURTH LOW-LEVELLER: It's not fair to those we represent.

ASSISTANT [*to* FIRST *and* SECOND LOW-LEVELLERS]: I am sure you are much too mature to mind. [*He pushes* THIRD *and* FOURTH *in front of them*]

FIRST LOW-LEVELLER: No, I'm sorry. That won't do.

SECOND LOW-LEVELLER: It's the principle of the thing.

A DELEGATE: What is that noise?

[*All now look at the big Door, now glowing brilliantly. But is it responsible for that soft deep note?*]

The Singing Door

THE SAME DELEGATE: Remember the old saying:
> 'When the Door begins to sing,
> That's a sign of coming spring.'

GUARDIAN: We all know these old tales. But remember, there is no agreement about their origin.

ONE OF THE NEW GROUP: The First People left them for us as a signpost.

A DELEGATE: No. My father, and he was an expert in the field, said they were anonymous. They come spontaneously from the populace.

A DELEGATE: What is spring?

ANOTHER: They say that Outside it is beautiful in spring.

ANOTHER: What is beautiful? We all use the word, but what does it mean?

ANOTHER: Anything gets called beautiful.

ANOTHER: It was flowers and leaves. [*Holding up some paper flowers*] Like this.

GUARDIAN: We have flowers and leaves.

THE DELEGATE WITH THE FATHER: My father said spring was a metaphor.

ANOTHER: My grandfather who was an expert said that flowers and leaves Outside are not like this, they are made of flesh.

THE DELEGATES, VARIOUSLY: Oh how disgusting. Revolting. Horrible. Repulsive. Ugh!

DELEGATE WITH THE GRANDFATHER: My grandfather had the theory that the word spring meant when Outside was covered all over with live tissue in different colours. You know, like our flesh, but different.

A DELEGATE [*shuddering*]: Like a sort of cancer.

DELEGATE: That would take a lot of getting used to for a start.

ANOTHER: That's what I've always said. I mean, we take it for granted that Outside would be better than here. But, ugh, flowers and leaves made of flesh, living flowers and leaves, I mean to say. [*He looks as if he is going to be sick*]

FIRST LOW-LEVELLER: My father spent all his life studying the old sayings. His version of the spring verse is quite different.

SECRETARY: You have scholarship down on the Lower Levels? Yes, yes of course you do . . .

[SECRETARY *exchanges a tolerant grimace with the* CHAIRMAN]

FIRST LOW-LEVELLER: He said it should go:
'The Door will sing,
Then through it spring.'

THIRD LOW-LEVELLER: I like the other one better.

FIRST LOW-LEVELLER: Here, you two can't stay there. You can't be in front of us. I don't care for myself but it is an insult to the 56th Level.

FOURTH LOW-LEVELLER: We aren't moving back and that's final.

CHAIRMAN: I do hope you will forgive me intruding, but I have a suggestion. You can't have been Hereditary Exalted Chairman all your life without learning something of the arts of compromise. [*He whispers to* ASSISTANT]

The Singing Door

ASSISTANT: You move there... [*He pushes* FIRST LOW-LEVELLER *with* FOURTH]... and you there... [*He pushes* THIRD *with* SECOND]

[*There is violent scuffling and disorder*]

FIRST LOW-LEVELLER: I'm not going to be with him. Look at his hair, if there wasn't anything else wrong.

THIRD LOW-LEVELLER: He makes me sick.

THE DELEGATE WHO COMPLAINED OF THE NOISE BEFORE: I'm sorry but I can't stand it. I have always been sensitive to noise. [*This one runs out, left, hands clapped to ears*]

[*The Door, glowing brilliantly, is sending out a strong sweet sound*]

FOURTH PRECEPT: 'The Door will sing.'

ONE OF THIS GROUP: 'The Door is singing, chanting, ringing,
        The Door is shining, burning clear,
        Leave your prison, the time is here!'

DELEGATE WHOSE FATHER WAS AN EXPERT: That's not the right version. I'm sorry.

ANOTHER FROM THE GROUP: 'The Door will glow,
        It's time to go.'

SAME DELEGATE: No, that's wrong.

ANOTHER: No, it isn't, I've heard that version often.

[*A babble of quarrelling breaks out in the procession. At the same time, all the group near the door, including the* DOCTOR *and* MEDICAL ATTENDANTS, *press closer to it. The* ATTENDANTS, *at a sign from* FOURTH PRECEPT, *pick up the stretcher with* FIFTH PRECEPT]

GUARDIAN [*taking command of the procession*]: This is a procession of Peace. Peace, I tell you.

FIRST LOW-LEVELLER [*grabbing* SECOND LOW-LEVELLER *and pulling him beside himself*]: You belong here.

GUARDIAN: Arrest the Low-Levellers.

[GUARDS *come forward to arrest them, but the four* LOW-LEVELLERS *spring out of the procession and stand in a group facing the* GUARDS, *weapons at ready*]

FIRST LOW-LEVELLER: We'll blow the whole place up.

FOURTH LOW-LEVELLER: And don't think we don't mean it.

DOCTOR: This must be a mass hallucination. It's hypnosis. It's a trick.

[*The Door is now a flood of brilliant light, while from it comes a beautiful deep note*]

ONE OF THIS GROUP: 'The atoms dance,
　　　　　　　　　　The Door's on fire,
　　　　　　　　　　The electrons sing,
　　　　　　　　　　Now seize your chance.'

ANOTHER: 　　　　'Watch and wait,
　　　　　　　　　Know the time,
　　　　　　　　　A singing Door,
　　　　　　　　　That's the sign.'

FOURTH PRECEPT: Come on. [*He signals the* MEDICAL ATTENDANTS *to the Door*]

DOCTOR: Stop.

[*The* MEDICAL ATTENDANTS *stop with the stretcher at the Door. All this group press up close, almost touching the Door.*

The Singing Door

The DOCTOR *hangs back a little, but he is being drawn slowly forward*]

GUARDIAN: In the name of the Door I command you to disarm.

FIRST LOW-LEVELLER: Silly old fools. Scared. Like a lot of sheep.

SECRETARY: Not sheep. Ship. Scared like a lot of ship. Ship, plural of sheep.

SECOND LOW-LEVELLER: What's a sheep anyway? What's it matter?

SECRETARY: It matters very much. We must preserve standards. When we do eventually leave this Underplace and go out again, into Outside, then we'll need to know these things.

FOURTH LOW-LEVELLER: We don't even know what the Door is for. It's just there.

[*He rushes over and kicks the Door on the altar*]

THIRD LOW-LEVELLER: There, you see? Nothing happens.

[*He kicks the Door too. Stands defying it*]

Go on, punish me then!

FOURTH PRECEPT: 'A singing Door,
           That's the time . . .'

[*He walks into the blaze of the Door and disappears. The others of that group follow, the* MEDICAL ATTENDANTS *taking the stretcher through last*]

DOCTOR: I must be mad!

[*He goes into the Door like the others. A couple of people rush across from the left, ignoring the procession, going straight to the Door*]

THESE SHOUT: Are we too late?

[*They jump into the light and vanish*]

FOURTH LOW-LEVELLER: Did you see that? Did you?

[*He rushes across and jumps into the light.* FIRST LOW-LEVELLER *does the same. One of the* GUARDS *goes after him. But are we imagining it, or is the light slightly less, the deep note a little higher and fainter?*]

GUARDIAN [*he has noticed nothing*]: As Guardian of the Door, I command you, finally, to submit to me.

CHAIRMAN: As Exalted Chairman I order you to give yourselves up.

GUARDIAN'S ASSISTANT: According to Regulation 37d you have no alternative but to disarm.

SECOND LOW-LEVELLER: Silly old ships.

[*He throws his grenade at the computer. It explodes in smoke and flying fragments. There is indiscriminate scuffling, shouting.*
The Door is now fading rapidly, and the sound is nearly back to its normal low humming.
Order is being restored over by the altar. SECOND *and* THIRD LOW-LEVELLERS *are disarmed and under arrest. A delegate lies dead*]

CHAIRMAN: That's over. We didn't allow ourselves to be intimidated.

GUARDIAN: I'm delighted to see that my authority still has force. And now I must make a plea for clemency.

The Singing Door

CHAIRMAN: Of course, they were misguided, that's all. And perhaps we were not without faults ourselves. We are perhaps too ignorant of what goes on in the Levels below 50.

DELEGATES: Hear, hear.

CHAIRMAN: I move that we appoint a commission to investigate ways and means to strengthen our ties with the levels below 50.

ASSISTANT TO GUARDIAN: But where are the other two Low-Levellers?

DELEGATE: When it came to the point, they got scared!

CHAIRMAN: Doctor, take these two young people into your care, will you? I am sure you don't mind a couple of extra patients . . . Where is the Doctor? Where have they all gone?

A DELEGATE: I saw them all run through the light. I mean, through the Door. They ran through the singing . . . I saw them.

CHAIRMAN: You saw what?

THIS DELEGATE: I saw them. I saw what happened. They've escaped! They've got out. They've left this Underplace for Outside!

[*He runs to the Door and beats his hands on it, trying to press himself through*]

They are free, I tell you. Free, free, free!

CHAIRMAN: Guard, take this poor man to the hospital . . . where's the other guard? Oh never mind. And the two Low-Levellers as well.

[GUARD *takes this* DELEGATE, *and two* LOW-LEVELLERS *out left*]

THIS DELEGATE: But I did see it. I did. Oh why was I such a fool? Why did I forget? . . .

[*He recites as he is pulled out of sight*]
'If you miss the place and time,
The Door again will sing and shine.'

THE DELEGATE WITH THE FATHER: That's not how that goes. It should go like this:
    'The song was sung,
    The moment's gone,
    Light and sound together came,
    Those who did not catch the time,
    Must watch until it comes again.'

THE DELEGATE WITH THE GRANDFATHER: That's not the way my grandfather knew it . . . He said it should go like . . .

CHAIRMAN: Another time, please. Is everyone ready now?

[*He takes his place beside the* GUARDIAN. *The* ASSISTANT TO THE GUARDIAN *hands them both garlands, hangs more around their necks. Some music starts up*]

ASSISTANT: Lights down please.

[*The* TECHNICIANS *turn down the lights. The Door can be seen glowing faintly in the half dark*]

CHAIRMAN: There you are, the technicians have got the lighting right—I said they would.

THE END

Burn-up

DEREK BOWSKILL

CAST

12 VOICES

All applications to perform this play, whether by amateurs or professionals, should be addressed to Curtis Brown Ltd, 13 King Street, Covent Garden, London WC2E 8HU

Burn-up

The play should be presented with an emphasis upon modern rhythms and beats, with much use of ritualistic chanting, variety of pace, and volume. There should be live percussion throughout. Improvisation and mime should spring from the words and sounds. The stanzas in italics are intended to be sung in the beat idiom.

VOICE 1: It's all for Real.

2: It's all for Real.

3: Let's get where the action is.

4: Let's go where the action goes.

5, 6, 7: To-day
　I saw
　My first . . .

8: Major Public Heart Transplant.

9: Astronaut lost in space.

10: Mass Execution by Nerve Gas.

1, 2, 3: To-day
　I saw
　My first . . . [*They strain for sound; nothing comes*]

4, 5, 6: To-day
　I saw
　My first . . . [*As before*]

7, 8, 9: My first . . . [*As before*]

10: Nothing.

ALL: My first Nothing.

1, 2, 3: Get them! [*Referring derogatively to the rest of the cast*]
You name it.
I've done it.

ALL: DONE
THE
LOT.

4: We've been where the action is.

5: We've got what it had to give.

6: We've been everywhere—

ALL: BEEN EVERYWHERE.

7: We've seen everything—

ALL: SEEN EVERYTHING.

8: Done the lot.

ALL: Yeah!

9: Done the lot.

10: Been . . .

11: Seen . . .

12: Done the lot.

ALL: Yeah!

1: Been . . .

2: Seen . . .

3: Done the lot.

1: Done the transplant . . .

ALL: Heart ah—goes ah—boom—boom.

2: Done the astronaut . . .

ALL: Long time no-see.

3: Done the nerve-gas . . .

1–6: *Come and have a sniff.*
Have a sniff on me.
Baby have a sniff on me.

7–12: *Come and have a sniff.*
Have a sniff on me.
Baby have a sniff on me.

4: We've been where the action is.

5: We've got what it had to give.

6: We've been everywhere—

ALL: BEEN EVERYWHERE.

7: We've seen everything—

ALL: SEEN EVERYTHING.

8: Done the lot.

ALL: Yeah!

9: Done the lot.

10: Been . . .

11: Seen . . .

12: Done the lot.

ALL: Yeah!

1: Been . . .

2: Seen . . .

3: Done the lot.

4: Done the pile-up;

5: Done the drowning;

6: Done the strip!

7: Done the pile-up.

8: Done the drowning.

9: Done the strip.

10: And the pile-up . . .
Wasn't as good.

11: And the drowning . . .
Wasn't as big.

12: And the strip . . .
Was not hot.

ALL: WAS NOT HOT.

1: And the pile-up . . .
Was terribly cool.

Burn-up

2: And the drowning . . .
  Was terribly wet.

3: And the strip . . .

ALL: WAS NOT HOT.

4: Had no fire.

ALL: HAD NO FIRE.

5: What we want is

ALL: FIRE.

6: What we want is

ALL: FIRE.

7: What we want is

ALL: FIRE.

8: What we want is

ALL: FIRE.

9: What we want is

ALL: FIRE.

10: What we want is

ALL: FIRE.

11: FIRE.

ALL: FIRE.

12: FIRE.

ALL: FIRE.

ALL: FIRE. FIRE. FIRE.

ALL: Let's get where the fire is.
Let's go where the fire goes.

1: To-day

2: I had

3: My first

1, 2, 3: Burn-up.

ALL: BURN-UP BURN-UP BURN-UP BURN-UP
Biggaranna—foresfiran—notazell [*Run together very fast*]

4: Bigger than a forest fire [*Articulated very carefully*]

ALL: AND HOT...
AS HELL.

5: Tonight, ladies and gentlemen, for your superior, sophisticated entertainment; your unlimited, extravagant pleasure; we present a few life-like snippets from the story of fire—a History of Burning.

7, 8, 9: *There were three children in the land of Israel—Shadrac, Meshak and Abed-Nego.*

6: There was also a great King. Nebuchadnezzar.

7, 8, 9: O King: Nebuchadnezzar, O King; live for ever; O King!
Nebuchadnezzar O King live for ever!

10: To-day, I command you, at the beating of the drum you shall fall down and worship my golden image.

Burn-up

7, 8, 9: O King: Nebuchadnezzar, O King; live for ever;
O King!
Nebuchadnezzar O King live for ever! [*Long pause*]
But we will not bow down and worship your golden image.
We will not bow down.

10: At the beating of the drum, bow down.
At the beating of the drum, bow down.
At the beating of the drum, bow down.
[*They stand still and there is silence*]

10: Since you will not bow down, Shadrac, Meshak and Abed-Nego, you shall be cast into the fiery furnace; heated seven times more than before.

[*Shadrac, Meshak and Abed-Nego, as if in chains, move to the furnace and a slow insistent beat begins*]

7, 8, 9: *There were three children in the land of Israel—Shadrac, Meshak and Abed-Nego.*

10: Bow down . . . Bow Down . . . Bow Down . . .
[*Beat continues to end of scene*]

11: Fire the furnace . . .
Hot . . . Hot . . . Hotter . . . Hotter . . . Hotter . . .

10, 11: Burn, you bastards, burn!
[VOICES 10 *and* 11 *vie with one another—getting louder and faster in impotent fury until they finally disintegrate into hysteria after their line together, as Shadrac, Meshak and Abed-Nego stand quite still and unmoved. There is silence. Pause.*]

12: But that was in Africa—ages ago.
In England it was really quite different.

1: If you're rich—because I'm not—you're a witch.

2: If you're clever—because I'm not—you're a witch.

3: If you're different—because I'm not—you're a witch.

ALL: You're a witch—you're a witch—you're a witch!

4: WITCH-HUNT. She's a witch.

ALL: She's a witch. She's a witch. She's a witch!

[VOICE 4 *points to* VOICE 6, *who is then sought out, possibly chased, and finally brought to a central position and forced to her knees*]

5: In the name of my name, with the power vested in me, I accuse you of witchcraft.

6: I am innocent.

5: In the name of the King, with the power vested in me, I accuse you of witchcraft.

6: I am innocent.

5: In the name of God, with the power vested in me, I accuse you of witchcraft.

6: I am innocent.

5: I offer you judgment by fire or water.

6: I choose water.

5: I offer you judgment by fire or water.

6: I choose water.

5: I offer you judgment by fire or water.

Burn-up

6: I choose water.

5: You have chosen, of your own free will, judgment by fire. If you burn you must surely be a witch and will die. If you do not burn—you will surely be a witch and must die. In the name of God, and with the power vested in me, I order this witch to be burned.
[*A slow chant begins*]

ALL: Burn the witch. Burn the witch. Burn the witch.
[*Continues. Above the prayer-type mumbling of 'burn the witch' can be heard:*]

5: In nomine patris, et filii et spiritus sancti.
[*The chant gains in strength and so does the drumming— getting louder and faster until it builds to a climax, at which point* VOICE 6 *screams and falls to the floor. There is silence and a pause*]

7: All that was a long time ago—and besides the wench is dead. They do it different in America.

ALL: *America. America. All we want is America.*
America. America. All we want is America.
[*During the singing,* VOICE 8 *becomes a Negro—perhaps using a mask—and as many of the cast as possible wear white head coverings. Then begins the chant. It is slow and quiet at first*]

ALL: White is good; black is bad; evil must be burned.
[*The chant continues and grows in speed and strength. Action accompanies it in which 8 is mercilessly badgered*]

ALL: KU—KLUX—KLAN. [*Whisper*]
KU—KLUX—KLAN. [*Stronger.*
This is followed by an explosion of drumming out of which the next lines emerge]

9, 10: What we want is FIRE.

11, 12: What we want is FIRE.

1, 2, 3, 4: What we want is FIRE.

ALL: What we want is FIRE!

ALL: Let's get where the fire is.
Let's go where the fire goes.

5: To-day

6: I had

7: My first . . .

5, 6, 7: BURN-UP.

ALL: BURN-UP!

8: Bigger than a fiery furnace.

9: Bigger than a burning witch-hunt.

10: Better than the KU-KLUX-KLAN.

11: And the biggest and best burn-up of all . . .

12: Fire for sacrifice—

ALL: Sacrifice!

1: Voodoo—the fire in the blood.

2: Voodoo—the fire in the soul.

3: Voodoo—the fire inside.

ALL: Voodoo—Voodoo—Voodoo—Voodoo!

4: *Take a friendship—twist it; break it.*

5: *Take a kind act—then suspect it.*

ALL: *All you need is—malice and envy.*
All you need is—greed and spite.

6: *Take an action—turn it, bend it.*

7: *Take a gesture—then reject it.*

ALL: *All you need is—malice and envy.*
All you need is—greed and spite.

8: Take a letter—any letter.

9: Take a letter—letter 'A'.

10: A says 'atred;

11: A says 'ateful;

12: A says anything you like.

ALL: *All you need is—malice and envy.*
All you need is—greed and spite.

1: Take a letter—any letter.

2: Take a letter—letter 'B'.

3: Be this;

4: Be that;

5: Be off.

6: B says B-anything you like.

ALL: *All you need is—malice and envy.*
All you need is—greed and spite.
All you need is—pins and cushions.
All you need is—candle light.

6: Take a cockerel in the left hand,
Take a sharp knife in the right.

7: Hold the cockerel in the left hand,
Hold a sharp knife in the right.

8: Strangle cockerel with the left hand.
Slash the cockerel with the right.

9: It's easy, when you try.

ALL: *All you need is—malice and envy.*
All you need is—greed and spite.
And a little candle-light.

10: There you have it,
Have Black Magic.

11: Not the chocolates,
Not the wrappings.

12: Just the dark and gooey centres.
Soft-centres:

1–3: Dark red jelly—black inside.

4–6: Black inside—dark red jelly.

7–9: Black—magic.

10–12: Voo—doo.

[*Then together*]

Burn-up

1–3 ⎫ Dark red jelly—black inside.
4–6 ⎬ Black inside—dark red jelly.
7–9 ⎨ Black—magic.
10–12 ⎭ Voo—doo.

[*The sequence is repeated until a point of dramatic climax is reached and all join in*]

ALL: Voodoo—Voodoo—Voodoo—Voodoo!

1: I know—it's 19.. [*Insert year*]
You're not superstitious.
Don't believe in witches.
Don't believe in Voodoo.
Or Black Magic.

2: Well, get this: 1970:
London; England; Sunday; March 29th; 10.30 p.m.
The initiation of a witch:
With fire.
[*Here, in low key, are presented some imaginary rites from the ceremony of initiating a witch. The ceremony should contain some of the following: smelling and sniffing; rubbing oils on the body; touching hands; symbolic eye-to-eye hypnosis; back to back dancing; erotic dance. The ritual should gain intensity and pace towards an explosive end. Towards the end of the ceremony all join in as follows—*
whispered at first and gradually gaining in speed and strength]

VOICES 1–6: Something's Burning . . .	7–1: I'm on Fire.
1–6: Something's Burning . . .	7–12: I'm on Fire.
1–6: Something's Burning . . .	7–12: I'm on Fire.
1–6: Fire . . .	7–12: Fire.
1–6: Fire . . .	7–12: Fire.

ALL [*double speed*]: Fire.   Fire.   Fire.   Fire.   FIRE!
[*Slow chant*] F.   I.   R.   E.
[*Drawn out cheer*] FIRE!

3: O.K. folks, let's try that again—from a Black Mass in London, 1970, to a Black Mass in Black Africa, West Africa, 1913. A young man is going through an initiation ceremony: Taboo. He will learn the tribe's general taboos and his own private taboos—above all, he will learn that to break a taboo is to die.
TABOO.

[*Drumming begins.*
VOICE 5 *plays the young initiate at whom all the instructions are aimed. He is powerless and afraid*]

4: Do not eat meat.

ALL: You must not eat meat.

4: Do not touch animals.

ALL: You must not touch animals.

4: Do not fill up a hole in the ground.

ALL: You must not fill up a hole in the ground.

4: Do not watch a death.

ALL: You must not watch a death.

4: Do not touch a corpse.

ALL: You must not touch a corpse.

4: And for you—your own personal, private, special taboo is never to see your own reflection.

ALL: Do not look: You must not look: [*Continues.*

The chanting builds and VOICE 5 *joins in. At an appropriate moment he inserts a new line, and everyone is shocked into silence*]

5: Do not spit. [*Silence. Pause. The pattern of response is picked up again*]

5: Do not spit.

ALL: You must not spit.

5: Do not smoke.

ALL: You must not smoke.

5: Do not shout.

ALL: You must not shout. [*Whispered*]

5: Do bring enough food.

ALL: You must bring enough food.

5: Do not take bottles or boxes.

ALL: You must not take bottles or boxes.

5: Do not disturb the doctor.

ALL: Do not disturb the doctor [*Continues in quiet rhythmic chant*]

6 [*speaking over the chant*]:
The man who turned the taboos upside-down was one Albert Schweitzer—doctor of Lambarene, West Africa. Self-styled jungle doctor. He did it by white magic—the magic of guts, courage and sheer bloody nerve.

7: 1913.
   In the middle of the jungle . . .
   The River Ogowe.
   750 miles long . . .
   Deep, fast and treacherous.
   On that river . . .
   A canoe,
   Paddled by natives.

8: On that canoe . . .
   Dr Albert Schweitzer.
   Age: 38.

   [*Drumming begins*]

ALL: *Through the jungle; up the river:*
   Past the mud huts; past the wood shacks:
   Past the palm trees; past the lemon trees:
   Past the rotten dying dead trees:

9: Meeting crocodile and hippopotamus
   And deadly stinging electric fish—
   Dr Albert Schweitzer.
   Age: 38.

ALL: Up the river: River Ogowe;
   Through the province: Province of Gabon;
   By the Hill Adolinanango,
   To the town of Lambarene.

   [*Drumming begins*]

ALL: *To the town of Lambarene. To the town of Lambarene.*
   To the town of Lambarene. To the town of Lambarene.
   Lambarene. Lambarene. Lambarene. Lambarene.
   Lambarene. Lambarene. Lambarene. Lambarene.
   [*A cymbal crash, or equivalent, to denote the actual jump to the river bank*]

10: To the town of Lambarene
   Arrived a doctor,
   With 30 cases of medicine.

ALL: He started to practise
   In a hen-house,
   A chicken coop.

11: When I arrived there was no patient.
   They were all frightened to death
   By the local fetishman,
   The witchdoctor.

12: [*shrieks and cries of* 'ju-ju' *from witchdoctor*]

11: My belief in the Historical Jesus
   Was good enough for me.
   One of my assistants—
   Trudi Boscher—
   Went out to meet the black witchdoctor.
   Signalled at him,
   Argued with him,
   Preached at him,
   Fixed him.
   And he went.
   [*Witchdoctor leaves*]
   And the sick and ailing came.

1: From time to time,
   A patient would arrive too late.
   He would operate—
   But the patient would die.
   And again would come
   The Black Witchdoctor.
   Back this time to claim the body.
   Back this time to claim the corpse.

2: Then another need for magic.
   His magic.
   His special brand of strong, white magic.
   To stand in the steaming jungle.
   With superstitious death all round,
   And challenge the might of the
   Taboo,
   The ju-ju,
   Was not easy.
   Listen . . .

12: Ju-ju. Taboo. [*Chanted against 3*]

3: Listen to the word of Historical Jesus.
   Listen to the voice of the Lord.
   I defy you, witchdoctor.
   I defy you, witchdoctor.
   Give way. [*Taboo chant style*]
   Give way.
   Give way.
   Voice of the Lord.
   Voice of the Lord.
   Listen to the word of Historical Jesus.
   Listen to the word of the Lord.

4: To the town of Lambarene
   Came a doctor—
   Albert Schweitzer.

5: Came a preacher—
   Albert Schweitzer.

4: He was a simple soul.

5: For a start
   He liked 'good' music.

Burn-up

4: *In the jungle, by the Congo*
   On the edge of hot Sahara
   Schweitzer played his grand piano—

ALL: *And would not kill.*

4: *Up the river, by the mountain*
   In the foetid, steaming jungle
   Schweitzer played at being surgeon—

ALL: *And would not kill.*

4: *In the shade of giant palm trees*
   In the land of crocodile
   Schweitzer played with leper children—

ALL: *And would not kill.*

4: *In the land of sleeping sickness*
   In the land of yellow fever
   Schweitzer found another Eden—
   Schweitzer found a place in Life—

ALL: And would not kill.
   And would not kill.
   And would not . . .
   Would not . . .
   Would not . . .
   Kill.

5: In Schweitzer land
   No anti-septic.

ALL: *Thou shalt not kill.*

6: In Schweitzer land
   No insecticide.

ALL: *Thou shalt not kill.*

7: In Schweitzer land
   No modern machines.

ALL: *Thou shalt not kill.*

8: Schweitzer would not kill a fly.

9: Schweitzer would not kill mosquitoes.

10: Schweitzer would not kill an ant.

11: Schweitzer would not kill.

12: He found his fire
    Burning in the heart of life.

ALL: Just try, for a day,
     His Reverence of Life.
     Just try, for an hour
     His Reverence of Life.
     Thou shalt not kill.

1: Schweitzer found the flame in all that lives.

2: Just try it, for a day.

3: But try it right—like Schweitzer.

4: Try this.

ALL: *Do not take life.*

5: And life for Schweitzer was in

6. *Blades of grass and flower petals,*

7: *Insect legs and bits of germs,*

8: *Poisonous snakes and bacilli,*

9: *Dogs with rabies—crocodiles.*

ALL: How the hell . . .
  Do you live . . .
  Like that?
  How the hell d'you live like that?

10: What a raving furnace
  In the heart of Schweitzer.

11: Get some fire, man.

12: Get some fire!

ALL: What we want is fire.
  What we want is magic.

1: I believe in the Historical Jesus. .

2: I believe in the Reverence of Life.

3: I believe in the Brotherhood of Pain.

4: Schweitzer reversed the usual success story.
  Had it all—gave it all away.

5: Oh, yes!
  This Schweitzer was no fool.

6: Played the organ—made a fortune.

7: Preached his sermons—made a fortune.

8: Wrote his books—made a fortune.

9: And what's more—won the Nobel Prize;
  Was given the Order of Merit—was given every
  Damned Oscar going—just like a Beatle

E

[*All scream*]

9: Before his time.
   Oh, yes—he was no fool.
   Try it, man,
   Try it for size.
   Get it first, then give it away.
   Get with it first, then be a square.

10: I believe in the Historical Jesus.
    I believe in the Reverence of Life.
    I believe in the Brotherhood of Pain.

11: Oh, yes—kinky too!
    The Brotherhood of Pain.
    Schweitzer believed there was good in Pain.
    The Bigger the Pain—the Better the Good.
    And this Pain brought people together.
    Just like sex.
    Try that, man,
    With your next bird—have a Pain Affair.

11: An Affair of Pain.

12: Jesus—Reverence—Pain.

1: But what's
   So cute
   About that?

ALL: *What we want is magic.*

2: I believe in the Historical Jesus.

ALL: *What we want is a Burn-up.*

3: I believe in the Reverence of Life.

ALL: *What we want is Fire.*

4: I believe in the Brotherhood of Pain.

5: Jesus—Reverence—Pain.

ALL: Give us an F—

6: Jesus [*Pronounced JEE-SUS*]

ALL: Give us an I—

7: Reverence [*Pronounced REV-RENCE*]

ALL: Give us an R—

8: Pain

ALL: Give us an E—

9: Jesus—Reverence—Pain

10: What have we got?

11: We've got Schweitzer.

12: We've got FIRE.

ALL: *We've got Schweitzer.*
We've got Fire.
We've got Schweitzer.
We've got Fire.
We've got Schweitzer.
We've got Schweitzer.
Schweitzer.
Schweitzer.
Schweitzer.
Schweitzer!

1: It is in the heart of men like Schweitzer
Where this fire is.

2: OK. He was a nut-case.

3: OK. He was round the bend.

4: OK. He was another Hitler.
But . . .
So what?

5: He had guts.

6: He had GO.

7: He had FIRE.

8: More than me, man.

9: More than you.

10: More than all of us.

11: And he was an old man of 90.

12: If what you want is FIRE.

1: Then get burning, man—
Burn inside.

2: Just like Schweitzer—
Burn inside.

3: 'Cos that's for real.

4: It's all for real.

5: That's where the action is.

6: That's where the fire is.

7: That's how the action goes.

8: That's how the fire goes.

9: Let's get where the fire is.

10: Let's go where the fire goes.

11: Today . . .
 I had . . .
 My first . . .
 [*Pause*]

12: Burn-up.

ALL: Burn-up. Burn-up. Burn-up. Burn-up.
 FIRE. FIRE. FIRE. FIRE. F. I. R. E. FIRE!

THE END

Weevils in My Biscuit

CHARLES SAVAGE

CAST

8 MALE VOICES
4 FEMALE VOICES

All applications to perform this play, whether by amateurs or professionals, should be addressed to Felix de Wolfe Associates, 61 Berkeley House, 15 Hay Hill, London W1X 7LH

Weevils in My Biscuit

SCENE: *A high rostrum represents the profile of an eighteenth-century boat: gang planks, ladders, ropewalks, canvas. The floor level in front is the quay: bollards, anchor posts, loading tackle. The men wear simple matelot gear, with manifold hat and quick wig changes. The women wear large skirts and shift shirts, with plenty of colour.*
V = *Male voice*
VF = *Female voice*
As the play begins, a steady drumbeat is heard as the actors enter and spread over the performing area.

V1: Rule, Britannia. Britannia Rules the Waves!

V2: King of the Seas . . .

V3: The sea-dogs of England . . .

V4: The British Fleet . . .

VF5: The Senior Service . . .

VF6: Salute the Mariners of England!

V7: High Lords of the High Seas . . .

V1: Her Majesty's Royal Britannic Navy!

[*Pause. Drum roll, then drumbeat stops*]

VF8: But where do we begin?

VF9: Noah.

VF8: Noah?

VF9: Noah, Noah's Ark.

V10: But he wasn't English!

V2: Alfred the Great.

V3: No, earlier. King Canute.

VF5: Canute? Canute and the Waves, you mean?

V3: Yes.

V1: Oh, hardly.

VF11: Richard the Lion-Heart, the Crusader King.

V12: The naval blockade and the Siege of Acre.

V1: Of course, Richard I was the Father of the Navy!

V2: But they weren't English ships . . .

V1: Oh.

VF5: King John? Now he really *is* the Father of the English Navy.

V4: Surely not? King John was a bad King.

VF5: Maybe, but he issued shipping charters to certain sea towns.

V12: Telling them that they had to supply ships at their own cost for 15 days a year.

VF5: Precisely. Take the town of Hastings:

V10: 'Also are ye to provide for fifteen days six shippes each to be manned by twenty-one men and one gromet.'

V2: Gromet? What was a gromet?

V10: Gromet—half man, half boy.

Weevils in My Biscuit

v1: Yes, well . . .

vf5: King John had a navy of 57 ships.

vf8: Manned by 1,000 men.

vf9: And 57 gromets.

v2: But only for 15 days.

v1: Then King John died.
[*Short pause*]

v12: Requiescat in pace, Johannes.
[*Pause*]

vf11: And what happened to the Royal Navy?

v10: It was disbanded. All the King's ships were sold.

vf5: Back to where we started.

v2: Until Henry V, the Hero King.

v3: 1415.

v1: Battle of Agincourt.

v4: 'Once more unto the breach,' etc. . . .

v1: Don't mock the dead.

v3 [*drumbeat to sound like horses' hooves*]: 'By the fastest horse, word is sent throughout the length of the land that all truehearted men who love well both their king and countrie are to repair straightway to Southampton, there to embark on board ship in preparation for the invasion of France.'

ALL: France!

[*Drum keeps going, underlying rhythm of the poem*]

V2: Fair stood the wind for France
    When we our sails advance
    Nor how to prove our chance
    Longer will tarry,
    But putting to the main
    At Caux, the mouth of Seine,
    With all his martial train
    Shall land King Harry.
    [*v2 takes crown to highest place at back of rostra*]

Song sung by V2

Our king went forth to Normandie
With grace and might and chivalry
Our God for him worked wonderously
Wherefore England may call and cry
Deo Gratias, Anglia,
Redde pro Victoria. [*Drumbeat*]

7 VOICES [*actors finger-click the rhythm*]:
Henry Five died in bed
Henry Six ruled instead
Back and forth in Civil War
Now it goes to Edward Four
Wicked Richard, dirty dick,
Tries a low-down rotten trick
Kills off Henry, Eddy's dead
Now the crown should grace his head.
Little Eddy in the Tower
Finds it isn't children's hour.
Wicked Richard will not yield
So he's killed at Bosworth Field.
Henry Seven dies in State
Leaves the crown to Henry Eight.

Weevils in My Biscuit

Henry, Edward, Mary, Liz [4 *beats*]
What a long, long reign hers is.

VI: No, hold it now, we'd better break
We've reached the age of Francis Drake.

V3: 1587 England. The Queen: Elizabeth I.

VF5: 1587 Spain. The King: Philip II.

V4: Philip to Elizabeth:

V12: 'Señorita Elizabetha gracious Queen of the green-land England—soon to be a Spanish province—you will please to do me the honour with your most beautiful hand in marriage. Posto Scripto: Please find enclosed, one ring, value, 200 crowns.'

V4: Elizabeth to Philip:

VF11: 'We thank you for your letter and the offer contained therein. Never will we—'

V6: The Royal 'we'—

VF11: 'entertain one singular thought in the way of marriage to yourself. The ring we will retain and remain your eternal enemy. Elizabeth Regina.'

V6: Result—WAR.

VI: War on the High Seas . . .

VF8: The destruction of Spanish treasure fleets . . .

V2: Capture of Spanish trading stations . . .

V7: Acts of daring and piracy.

V10: The Elizabethan Navy—founded on raiding and trading!

v7: Sir John Hawkins. He appears to have had a private navy permanently at the ready.

v6: Walter Raleigh, Martin Frobisher, Charles Howard of Effingham, Lord Admiral.

vF9: And Francis Drake.

v7: 1587: Spain prepares a massive fleet for an invasion of England.

v6: 1587: The English ships far from home, chase after Spanish gold.

v2: If the Armada had invaded 3 months earlier we'd probably all be Spanish colonials today.

v1: But Drake dropped into Cadiz and singed the King of Spain's beard and the rumours started.

v6: Drake is gathering his forces . . .

vF9: Drake has appeared off Calais . . .

v7: Drake has sunk so many ships . . .

v6: Drake plans to invade Brazil . . .

v10: Drake is off the Isle of Wight . . .

vF5: Drake's here, Drake's there . . .

v1: Drake. Drake. Drake. DRAKE!

v7: With a man like Drake you didn't need a Navy!

vF9: And in fact we didn't have a Navy when the Armada sailed.

v2: The Armada, a fleet of 130 ships.

Weevils in My Biscuit

v4: Forty-two thousand fighting men.

v6: 123,790 canon balls.

v7: And 180 good Catholic priests.

v1: The invincible Armada.

v12: But the British Navy beat it!

vf11: Or was it the English weather?

v7: Certainly not—it was a great naval victory.

v12: But more Spanish treasure boats reached home safely than ever before.

v1: And now more new Spanish colonies,

v2: and French . . .

v3: and Dutch and

v4: Belgian . . .

v6: and Portuguese . . .

v12: And even defeat at sea for Francis Drake . . .

[*Song: 'Drake's Drum', by Sir Henry Newbolt*]

vf8: So Queen Elizabeth founded the Navy?

v1: You can't really have a *Mother* of the English Navy!

v2: No, motherhood was one thing that Elizabeth I never achieved.

vf11: As far as you know . . .

vf5: Move on?

V1: RIGHT.

SEVERAL VOICES: Come on, Lizzie, change the order
　　　　　　　　Something's coming o'er the border.

V6: 　　　　　James I with Highland flings
　　　　　　Establishes the Stuart Kings.

[*Universal groan*]

V4: And what did you do for the Navy?

V6: I repaired my Royal dockyards—but I never had no ships to put in 'em.

V1: Next?

ALL: Cheerful Charlie next in line
　　　Claims, . . .

V10: . . . I rule by right divine!

V4: And what did you do for the Navy, your Majesty?

V10: I invented the first Lord High Admiral.

V4: Who?

V10: My friend here, the Duke of Buckingham. My best friend, he was.

V4: You?

V7: Yes—but some sailors murdered me at Portsmouth.

V4: Why?

V7: I forgot to pay the sailors.

V6, V12: He forgot to pay the sailors!

V4: That's scandalous.

v10: But I think I might claim to be the Father of the British Navy.

vf5: Witness the Venetian Ambassador:

v12: 'Most of the ships in the English Fleet be old and rotten and barely fit for service.'

vf11: Witness:

v6: 'There is a loathing amongst every kind of people against all service in H.M. ships and fleets.'

vf9: Witness:

v3: 'Foul winter weather, naked bodies and empty bellies make the men call the King's service worse than galley slavery.'

v4: Well?

v10: But I won victories, built three new ships.

v4: Next . . .

3 voices: House of Commons very cross
        Olly Cromwell voted boss.

v1 [*shouts*]: Civil War!

3 voices: Saying prayers and chanting psalms
        Cromwell's forces take up arms.

[*Entire cast line up in marching order two by two. Actors playing Charles I and Cromwell at front. They stamp the rhythm*]

ALL [*sung to the tune 'The Church's One Foundation'*]:
We are the model army
Like Cromwell's army we.

There is no drink, we do not swear
Nor is there blasphemy.
When we sail into battle
Against Charles the Cavalier
Then God shall be our leader
And Christ shall be our cheer.

3 VOICES: House of Commons with a chopper
Kills off Charlie good and proper

ALL: Chop! Chop! Chop! [*Cheer*]

V1: Cromwell for King, the people cry—

V2: But the crown he will not try.

V1: People restive, plotting starts—

V2: Cromwell—Olly fast departs.

SEVERAL: Restoration—bring back King
Charlie Two's the name we sing.

[*The rhythm changes*]

V2: Aye, Charlie II for fun and games
The Navy's in the hands of my brother James.

V1: James II, while James, Duke of York,
Kept a mouldy Navy on mouldy salt pork.

V7: Hey, wait a minute, we've left out heaps—
Nobody mentioned Samuel Pepys.

VF5: Samuel Pepys, famous for his diary.

VF11: July 1st 1660: Pepys appointed Secretary for the Affairs of the Admiralty.

Weevils in My Biscuit

v4: 'I find the Navy in a very sad condition and money must be raised for it.'

v12: There was a Navy debt of over one million pounds.

vf8: The Navy was costing three-quarters of the National Income.

v7: Questions in Parliament, a public scandal.
Worse still, the men are never paid.

v3: Desertion, riots in ports. But still no pay.

vf9: One captain was reported to have sailed up and down the coast of Ireland for 2 years waiting for money from the Admiralty to pay off his crew.

vf5: So Pepys stepped in.

v1: Everything was tightly listed, detailed, timetabled.

v2: First-rate warship: 98 guns, 778 men.

vf9: Four hundred of these were special 'mariner' soldiers.

vf8: Pepys had invented the marines!

v10: Recruitment was a problem—but the Press-gang system defeated even Pepys.

vf5: Nobody wanted to serve in the Navy.

v4: 'Although the King's wages be better than merchantmen's yet the King's service is shunned for the men are never paid.'

v1: He didn't give up. If there was no pay forthcoming then conditions on board could be made more attractive.

v4: 'Englishmen, and more especially seamen, love their bellies above everything else, and therefore it must always be remembered in the management of the victualling of the Navy to make any abatement in the quantity or agreeableness of the food is to render them sooner disgusted with the King's service than any other one hardship that can be put upon them.'

vF11: With that in mind Pepys set up a Victualling Board.

v7: David Gawden, grocer, got the monopoly for food supply.

vF11: But he went broke.

v7: The Navy owed him £200,000.

vF11: In any case his food was rotten and mouldy.

vF8: You know they used to call his foodstore 'The Old Weevil Depot'.

vF9: And the rats were too fat to run away.

v1: But Pepys didn't give up.

v1: Good. But Pepys was hardly the Father of the English Navy!

v2: Decidedly not. It was a bad time at sea.

v3: The Dutch sailed up the Thames and burnt our best ships.

vF8: London was thrown into a panic.

vF5: Rumours of invasion.

v3: And where was the King? The King? The King?

v4: 'I was told today that the Court is as merry as ever; and

Weevils in My Biscuit

that the night the Dutch burned our ships the King, with his brother the Duke of York—

v2: Admiral of the Fleet—

v4: 'Did sup with my Lady Castlemaine and the Duchess of Monmouth—and after they were mad in a new sport of hunting moths. Which sport it is reported they executed most graciously to music.'
[*Butterfly nets, chasing, and music-minuet*]

v1: Next! Next! William III, William of Orange.
[*Rhythm*]

v3, v2: Jamey II was a wily old bird
But he had to abdicate to William Third.
William dies and in his stead
Poor Queen Anne—sssh, Queen Anne's dead!
Next two Georgies count for nowt.
Hardly English, more like Kraut.
1760 and Georgie Three
Now Britannia Rules the Sea!

v7: At last a father for the English Navy: George Third!

vf5: The great age of Rodney, Howe, Nelson.

vf11: Naval victories—Trafalgar, the Nile, the Glorious First of June.

v2: Captain Cook, exploration and new colonies.

v1: We also lost a colony—America . . .

v2: They'll come back.

vf5: Vast wealth from overseas trade.

v6: A permanent standing Navy, staffed by first-class officers.

v12: What about the mutinies: Nore, Spithead, Mutiny on the *Bounty*?

vf11: New fast frigates and heavy gunned warships.

v12: Appalling conditions on board, rats, lice, cockroaches.

vf9: Bad beer, mouldy pork.

v7: But the world over the British Navy was respected as Lord of the High Seas.

v1: 1780.

vf5: King George Third.

v3: Not officially mad yet . . .

v7: And in 1780, Your Country Needed You.

vf11: Why?

v1: Bad relations with France.

v6: The common soldier and sailor were regarded on the same level as the prostitute and beggar.

v10: Many sailors were recruited from the prisons.

v6: Villages inflicted with no-goods and idiots sent them as a gift to the local Navy depot.

v12: 'Herewith one Francis Juniper of Cuckfield, a drunken troublesome fellow without a coat to his back. We wish you good fortune with this fellow and do guarantee him free of the smallpox and the itch.'

vf11: In 1780 there were 490 ships in the Navy in which 98,000 men were giving service.

Weevils in My Biscuit

v4, vf9: Press, Press, run for your lives. Run. The Press-gang come.

vf9: Run for your wives. Run, run, run. The Press-gang come.

v1: At the cry of 'Press-gang' the street emptied in a flash.
[*All exit except* vf5 *and* v6]

v6: Make way, make way there for his Royal Majestie's Naval Recruition Officers, make way.

vf9, vf8 [*song*]: For God's sake, laddie
    Run, run, run
    The Pressman he doth
    Come, come, come
    For the sake of your life
    Now run, run, run
    For the sake of your wife
    Do run, run, run
    The Press is here
    The Press is here
    So laddies everywhere
    Just run, run, run
    Run, run.

v2: Shoreham, Sussex. 'The Press-gang besieged the town here for 10 hours, but never saw a single man—all they captured was one woman in breeches.'

vf11: But they captured 8 smugglers on the way home.

v2: The Gangers swooped without any warning.
Nancy Clarke...

vf5: 'At midday I left my husband, he being taken with a great sickness to go fetch the Parson to him, I thinking his time had come. On my return his bed were empty and he gone nor never to this day have I seen he since.'

v1: But England is at war with France, the ships must be manned.

vf8: It wasn't easy for the Press-gangs. Press-master Henry Smith from Nottingham . . .

v12 [*reads*]: 'To their Lordships at the Admiralty, London.
Sirs, my trouble is increased mightily every day for the violence that I meet with on attempting an impressment. I am tormented everyday, the mayor objecting, men complaining, all entreating, I cannot impress here.

I can neither eat nor drink nor sleep, but I am molested. But yesterday my gangers were set upon with cudgels and knives. I beg your Lordships' mercy and ask that I may be moved off from this town of coarse and unmannerly people.'

vf8: Enclosed with his letter Henry Smith sent the Admiralty a bill for expense.

v12: 'To a surgeon for dressing wounds received by the gangs in frays—18/9d.
For bailing myself and three of my gang from gaol—£1.13.6.
Fee at court—10/3d.
To a constable for withdrawing an action against one of my men who had in error captured the said constable—£7.7.0.'

v7: The Press-gang met with better success in the villages.

vf8: But the best place of all for pressing was around the merchant docks in London.

Weevils in My Biscuit

v2: That's him—that's our man, the small fat fellow there!
[*This scene is mimed out with a 'fray' as the man is pressed*]

v6: 'As I crossed Tower Wharf, with my delightful companions, a squat tawny fellow with a hanger by his side and a cudgel in his hand came up to me calling.'

v1: 'Yo ho, brother! You want to come along with me?'

v6: 'As I did not like his appearance I quickened my pace in the hope of ridding myself of his unpleasant company; upon which he blew a whistle—'
[*1st man blows whistle and 2 others spring out*]
'—and immediately two other sailors sprang up before me, laid hold of me by the collar and began to drag me along.'
[*Improvised sequence—rough handling, girls transfer allegiance, man is dragged up ramp and clapped in irons*]

v4: Hear ye, Hear ye, Hear ye all this advertisement for His Majestie's Royal Navy.

v2: 'All true-blue British Hearts of Oak, who are able and no doubt willing to serve their good King and Country on board his Majestie's ships are hereby invited to serve on board the ships now lying at Portsmouth, Plymouth, Chatham and Sheerness, under the command of Vice-Admiral Geary.'

v3: Dreary Geary.

v2: 'Rear Admiral George Lord Edgcumbe,'

v4: Razorbumbe

v2: 'and Commodore Hills——'

v5: Pills.

V2: 'All seamen will receive three pounds bounty and ordinary seamen two pounds with conduct money, and their chests, bedding, etc., sent carriage free.'

VF8: Of course, they never got the money.

VF9: And their baggage was stolen at the harbour.

V2: 'N.B. For the encouragement of discovering seamen that may be impressed a REWARD of two pounds will be given for able and 30/- for ordinary seamen. Success to his Majesty's Navy! With health and limbs to the jolly tars of Old England. God Save the King.'

V10: 'Wanted:'

V12: 'Englishmen willing to defend their country against the attempts and designs of our natural enemies, the FRENCH, who intend in this year to invade our old England, to murder our gracious King, as they have done their own; to make whores of our wives and daughters and teach us nothing but the damned art of murdering one another.'

BOSUN [V3]: All aboard! All aboard! Prepare to sail!

CAPTAIN [V1]: 'My dear wife Betsy, Today arrived words from their Lordships at the Admiralty. We are under orders to sail. As I write these words the men make their last fond farewells on shore to wives, sweethearts, mothers, babes in arms. My truest affection and duty to you my dearest, and my thoughts for our children.
                        Yours,
                Alexander Coleman. Captain.'

BOSUN [V3]: Prepare to sail!

CAPTAIN [V1]: Mr Bosun?

Weevils in My Biscuit

BOSUN [v3]: Aye sir!

CAPTAIN [VI]: Tell those lubbers if they are not aboard immediately I'll have them stretched to the gratings and flogged.

BOSUN [v3]: Aye sir! Hey you lot, shake your bloody sea-legs and get aboard! And get straightway and wash yourself seein' as to the company you keep!

CAPTAIN [VI]: Mr Bosun?

BOSUN [v3]: Sir!

CAPTAIN [VI]: Give order to weigh in the anchor.

BOSUN [v3]: Sir! Weigh anchors! Anchors a-weigho!

SAILOR [v2]: Anchor team above. Let's have you.

v12: Wait! Wait! Do you mean that this is the Great Age of the British Navy?

v2, v3: Yes, of course. Anchors a-weigho!

v4: But what about the Iron bottoms?

vF5: Don't be vulgar!

v4: I mean the Iron boats, the first big battleships.

v6: The Great Age of Steam.

v2: Nonsense, not a patch on sail.

v3: Quite, whoever heard of the Victorian Navy?

v2: Make sail!

vF5: But you can't ignore the *Cutty Sark*, the Calcutta sea-clippers.

v3: They were mere Traders.

V10: I've got it, I've got it. You are forgetting, the Sailor King!

V2: Yachts!

V10: I beg your pardon?

V2: Yachts, mere pleasure boats. Let us not compare Trafalgar with Cowes—

VF8: Submarines!

V3: How low can you get?

V12: H.M.S. *Ark Royal*, *Eagle*. Don't forget the British Navy role in the World War II——

V2: Sssh! They're in the knacker's yard now.
[*Pause*]

V1: Well, what's wrong with the Navy to-day?

V3: This is not a political programme!

VF9: Let's get on with it. It's obvious the Golden Age of the British Navy is Nelson and Trafalgar. That's when ships were ships.

V2: Carry on, Bosun!

BOSUN [V3]: Make sail! Anchors aweigh!

ALL WOMEN: Three cheers for Nelson and the British Navy!

VOICE 1: Britannia Rules the Waves!

VF5: So let Nelson's men have the final word! Listen . . .

V3: 'The hotter the war, the sooner the peace. When everything is cleared, the ports open, the tapers lighted, the guns run out, then we give three such cheers as are only to be heard on a BRITISH man-of-war.'

v1: 21st October.

v4: 1805.

v6: 'ENGLAND EXPECTS THAT EVERYMAN WILL DO HIS DUTY THIS DAY'

v7: VICTORY FOR NELSON'S *VICTORY*!'

v10: The Battle of Trafalgar!

v12: And we won!

v2: In spite of the weevils in our biscuits!

Song

BOSUN [v3]: Our shippe went a sailing out over the Bar.
   Weigh for Rio!
   We've pointed her bow to the Southern Star
     An' we're bound for the Rio Grande.

CHORUS: Then away, boys, away!
   Weigh for Rio!
   The biscuits is weevily,
     The salt pork is tough,
   An' we're bound for the Rio Grande.

BOSUN [v3]: We've a bloody good ship an' a bloody good crew.
   Weigh for Rio!
   But we don't like the grub, no I'm damned if we do,
     An' we're bound for the Rio Grande.

CHORUS: Then away, boys, away!
    etc. etc.

BOSUN [v3]: Oh, farewell to Sally and farewell to Sue.
    Weigh for Rio!
    An' you on the pierhead it's farewell to you,
    An' we're bound for the Rio Grande.

CHORUS: Then away, boys, away!
    etc. etc.

THE END